to
Ann Jerome
with
Best Wishes,
Mark Langerno

FILING DYNAMICS

developments in color coding for filing systems

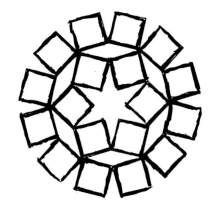

FILING DYNAMICS

developments in color coding

for filing systems

by
Donald T. Barber, CA, CRM, CDP
and
Dr. Mark Langemo, CRM

MARSDALE PUBLISHING CO.

Emeryville, California
and
Toronto, Ontario

Marsdale Publishing Co., Ltd.
    3300 Powell St., Emeryville, California 94608
    3080 Yonge St., Toronto, Ontario M4N 3N1

Published 1987.
Printed by Dai Nippon Printing Company, Ltd.,
Tokyo, Japan
95 94 93 92 91 90 89 88 87   5 4 3 2 1

Barber, Donald T., CA, CRM, CDP
Langemo, Dr. Mark, CRM

Filing Dynamics—developments in color coding for
filing systems.

Includes index.

Library of Congress Catalog Card Number: 87-60316
ISBN 0-941151-00-X

ACKNOWLEDGMENTS

Psychologists tell us that we are part of everything we have done and thought. In a way this book is a reflection of that truth. Over the years the authors have talked with many people, seen many systems, and have tailored many record systems to particular needs. Each and every one of them was another learning experience. Each added just a little more to the background of our understanding. Based on this we can speak from the heart. Every word is the truth as we see it. The shortcomings are ours; the merits belong to those who taught us.

But who are they? How do we acknowledge their contributions to this book? It is a problem for which we do not have an answer. We can only hope that those who know us and who have directly and indirectly taught us will accept our thanks. We are grateful to them.

However, there are a few who can be named who have assisted in the wearisome work of typing and retyping copy, editing, pagination and all the other drudgery that goes with printing and publishing a book. First is Yolanda Noronha who typed and retyped copy on our word processor about fifty times; and then there is Sally Leete who pulled it all together about fifty times; and then there is Harley Leete who kept correcting and editing the copy. Not to mention our editorial board who kept suggesting new chapters and new ideas. Your work is appreciated. Many thanks.

INTRODUCTION

At this time, when great technological advances are necessary to handle the growing mass of business information, a book on paper-based filing systems may seem an anachronism. Yet it is obvious that, despite years of talk of a paperless society, paper continues to be a vital and necessary business tool. This fact has long been understood by volume users of paper. Their need for efficiency has been responsible for dramatic developments in paper-based filing systems. This book is the story of those developments.

The narrative begins with removing folders from drawer files and storing them on shelves. This means changing index tabs from the top to the side of the folder. Next, color-coded labels exploit the visibility of side tabs, leading to a spectacular increase in file room efficiency. And finally, by storing folder identification data and movement history on a microcomputer, and putting OCR-readable labels on folders, a full folder tracking and control system becomes possible.

The essential message is simple: business will naturally use such technology as laser imaging and microfilm to eliminate *unnecessary* paper. Just as naturally, the tools and techniques described here will be used to control *necessary* business paper as efficiently as is other business information.

This is not a typical text book. It is written for busy people with an interest in the basics of paper-based filing techniques. We trust that it will be a modest contribution to the ongoing search for excellence in business record keeping.

> Donald T. Barber
> Dr. Mark Langemo

TABLE OF CONTENTS

This describes the use of color coding and a microprocessor to achieve Filing Control of paper records. It also deals with the many tools available to the skilled manager to meet specific needs of a records system. A typical application is described.

The Association of Records Managers and Administrators publishes a comprehensive guide to alphabetic filing. An alternative is the simple set of rules used in the telephone directory.

This is a discussion of the different color-coded filing systems in general use. It tells how and why they were developed, their advantages and disadvantages.

In subject filing, the classic problem is to assign reference numbers to subjects in the same alphabetical sequence as they are arranged in the index. When the computer concept is adopted, this is no longer necessary and file reference is simplified by using color-coded File Locator Numbers.

This brief description of the operation of the microprocessor tells how it is used to control the records system through a Menu of Functions. The functions are described, showing how they are used in the system.

VI THE FILING SURVEY

Since the requirements of every filing system are different, a survey is needed to discover the facts. Here we have suggestions and ideas on how to do this. Then, by analyzing the facts, we develop the most suitable records management system. We also measure its cost effectiveness.

VII THE EVOLUTION OF RECORDS MANAGEMENT

By stepping back to gain perspective, we better understand the present state of the art in records management. This is a short summary of the step-by-step developments that have occurred over the years to achieve filing control.

VIII THE IMPORTANCE OF PEOPLE

An atmosphere of trust, respect and good humor is a vital pre-requisite for a system that truly works.

APPENDIX A — VARIOUS TYPES OF FILES

APPENDIX B — VARIOUS TYPES OF FOLDERS AND GUIDES

SUGGESTED READING

A short list of books that are classics of records management. They will broaden anyone's understanding and are recommended reading.

INDEX

TECHNOLOGY IS A DECEITFUL MASTER...

...and its hoped-for benefits are often accompanied by shockingly high costs in money and effort. This is particularly apparent in filing systems, where many companies have discovered, to their sorrow, that microfilming and other high-tech methods did not improve their record-keeping, but added disproportionately to administrative costs. Meanwhile, golden opportunities go begging. The story of developments in paper-based filing efficiency is simple, but it contains treasure, as many wise users can attest.

Most transactions are recorded on paper because it is the least expensive, most user-friendly medium for the recording, storage and retrieval of information. If your paper-based system is a mess, beware of solutions that just move the mess to a computer. Problem solving is different from that. It is clearly understanding functional requirements and selecting, from a universe of possibilities, the method with the best productivity-to-cost ratio for getting the job done. Many of these methods will continue to be paper-based, as far as we can see into the future.

John Stubbs
Lombard, Illinois

I

FILING CONTROL

This book deals with the control of file folders that contain hard-copy paper documents. Folders are used almost universally in offices to house paper for all kinds of transactions. They come in various sizes, shapes and kinds — letter, legal, metric, expansion, with and without fastening devices, etc. Almost everyone uses them — doctors, lawyers, accountants, and businesses of every kind and size.

THE PAPERLESS OFFICE

You may say this is all "old hat." With the paperless office just around the corner, are we polishing the brass on a sinking ship?

Well, the truth is that paper is with us now and will be for a long time. The increasing volume of documents produced day after day by ubiquitous copiers, word processors, and advanced data-processing equipment adds up to a growth that strains the capacity of our paper mills and forests.

The consensus of expert opinion indicates that technology does not threaten the active, paper-based records management business. And so our mission is to improve hard-copy filing systems, make them cost effective and, above all, enable management to exercise control of the filing process.

LOOKING AT THE PROBLEM

Somehow, filing systems seem so straightforward, simple, and elementary that the subject doesn't appear to deserve management attention. After all, you may say, filing systems have been around a long time and, if there were a better way to file documents, someone would have discovered it long ago. It could be argued that if filing is in a mess, no one could have found a better way. The easy answer is to buy another cabinet or hire another clerk. One solution that is talked about is to change all the paper to microfiche and, somehow, everything will come up rosy.

Another is to record it all in a computer and throw away the paper. Well, in special situations, such a solution may be the right one. However, there is another approach. It is proving effective, and pays handsome dividends, in large and small companies. This is to take advantage of several cost-effective tools that have been developed for filing systems in the last few years. That is what this book is all about.

DIVIDING THE PROBLEM INTO PARTS

A well-known axiom states that the best solution to any large problem can be discovered by dividing it into parts. In this way, each segment can be studied and solved. By doing so, we rethink the problem. And as with any office process, we should keep asking ourselves, "How can we make use of that great modern wonder tool, the microprocessor?"

But let's face it, there is no magic wand that, by itself, solves all our records problems in a flash. Efficiency comes about by a series of steps — each contributing to and each reinforcing the other — until the final solution is reached.

WHY DO ANYTHING?

The first question to be asked about record keeping is "Why do anything?" The simple answer is, "Don't, if the filing system is A-OK." However, if there is a doubt, then a survey should be considered. These are questions that need to be asked:
- Are the files active?
- How active?
- Can some be transferred to dormant storage or destroyed?
- Is space a problem?
- Are lost or misplaced files a problem?
- Can folders, out of file, be located quickly?
- Is the index adequate?
- Is there provision for growth?
- Are files overcrowded?
- Is it simple and convenient to find a file, use it, and refile it?

The only way to find the answers is through a filing survey. This is discussed in Chapter 6, beginning on page 55.

DRAWER FILES ARE OFFICE ANTIQUES!

A good first step in achieving filing efficiency is to ask one easy question: "Are we using top-tab folders housed in drawer files?" Since horse and buggy days, drawer files have been the accepted way to file folders. And today many filing systems still follow tradition by using them. This is a sure sign that improvements can be made.

Why?

Because about twenty years ago a trend started that has been gaining strength ever since — a change from drawer to lateral or shelf filing using side-tab folders. There is a reason for this. There is a worthwhile saving of space when there are no drawers, because files go higher and aisles are narrower.

It is also more efficient because labor is saved, since drawers do not have to be pulled out or pushed in. And it is usually 25% faster. There is a growing trend to change over from drawer to lateral files using side-tab folders, and thus to save up to 40% of floor space.

SUSPENDED FILING

For a person sitting at a desk, with a limited number of files for reference or current action, a popular and convenient way to file is in suspended pockets in one or two drawers of a desk. Each pocket is used for loose paper or folders.

Suspended pockets are also used in two-drawer rollout cabinets behind desks. This kind of one-person, hands-on filing is probably best left alone, because personal habits are hard to change. This book is about filing systems that serve the whole office. A word of caution about large systems using suspended pockets: they are expensive and take up too much space.

ROLLOUT CABINETS

There is a lateral filing cabinet called a "rollout." Here drawers of the traditional file are arranged to pull out *sideways*. Interior designers often suggest these for a "modern" appearance.

Their main advantage is that top-tab folders in drawer files can be transferred to rollouts without changing folders. There are modest space savings because drawers do not pull out as far as formerly. However, for most filing systems, there is little to recommend rollouts.

LATERAL FILING HARDWARE

In response to demand for lateral or shelf filing, new and better equipment is now available. Two types of lateral files are in use: open systems without doors, and closed cabinets with doors and locks. The open system is most productive, and saves space. Structurally, it consists of posts, and open boxes that hang from rails. The boxes support folders, holding them upright. They are easily rearranged as the system expands or contracts.

With a closed system, shelves are welded into cabinets, making a solid unit, which comes with leveling feet and doors that serve as work shelves. Metal dividers keep the folders upright.

Every year, lateral cabinets return their purchase price in dollars saved from your staff's filing time.

LATERAL FILING WITH COLOR CODING

As discussed, starting twenty years ago, there was a shift from drawer to shelf filing, using side-tab folders. Color coding was introduced at the same time. This was natural, because the ends of folders were visible. Thus the way was opened for many developments in color coding. This is a story in itself!

COLOR CODING OF TERMINAL DIGITS

At first, color was used to code large numeric filing systems, dividing files into groups. This was done by arranging folders according to the last two digits. Two methods were used to color code terminal digits. One involved matching stripes. Here the folder side was divided into eleven equal parts. Beginning at the top, parts were assigned to the digits 0 through 9. The bottom position identified a repeat, such as 7 7. Corresponding to the particular digits, parts were printed in black, thus creating two bars for each two-digit section.

In the second method, distinctive colors were assigned to digits 0 through 9. The digits, with their color bands, were printed around the folder edge, corresponding to the two terminal digits. Misfiles were identified by mis-matched bars or colors. (See illustrations on pages 35 and 36.)

COLOR CODING SEQUENTIAL NUMBERS

These approaches to color coding were restricted by the inability of manufacturers to print more than two colors or stripes on a folder. Soon other approaches were developed. One was to print, in a sequence of operations, a series of numbers, for instance, from 00001 to 80000.

File clerks in these pictures can see and reach folders in all seven tiers of the hanging box files. Note that every number in this straight numeric system is readable. The installation shown occupies only 40% as much space as drawer cabinets housing an equal quantity of folders. These factors speed filing and finding and reduce clerical effort.

Each digit was printed, with its distinctive color block, on heavy paper. In a final operation, the number was cut out and glued around the edge of the folder. (This description is a simplification. Actually, numbers were printed ten-up on large sheets, so that each printing run yielded ten series of color-coded numbers.)

AN AMAZING INCREASE IN EFFICIENCY

When five or six digits of a number were color coded in this way, there was an amazing increase in filing efficiency. This was because a folder could easily be located by looking at the extreme edge. With a little practice, colors were "read" as numbers. Filing efficiency relates directly to the time it takes to locate a specific folder. Maximum efficiency is achieved when search time becomes almost instantaneous.

COLOR CODING RANDOM NUMBERS

Another method of manufacture was to print numbers on punched cards. The numbers required were punched into the cards. Then, in a series of sorting and printing operations, the digits, with their distinctive color blocks, would be printed. A final sort brought them into the correct sequence. The printed numbers were die-cut from the cards and glued around the edge of folders.

This was a great leap forward!

Folders with an incomplete series of reference numbers could be manufactured. Changeovers from top-tab to color-coded side-tab filing became easier. Now, new color-coded folders could be prepared in advance of the changeover, in the exact sequence, folder for folder, of those in use.

All digits of a number need not be color coded. For example, for 1478654, the last five digits, 78654, could be color coded and the prefix number, 14, printed in black.

AUTOMATIC MANUFACTURING

Next, there was a dramatic development in manufacturing color-coded folders. It was the automatic, high-speed application of pressure sensitive labels to folders. Here, blank folders are automatically fed onto a conveyor belt. They are exactly positioned and pass under fourteen computer-directed high-speed labelers. Labels can be applied in any order — sequential, terminal digit, random, or whatever.

In the process, labels are wrapped around the edge of the folder. Blank folders become color coded as if by magic! By printing bar codes on labels, they are made machine readable by hand-held wands. This enables total records control by a microprocessor. More about this later.

HOW MUCH COLOR CODING?

A word of caution about color coding. Avoid overdoing it. Too much is too much. The main purpose is to identify folders so they can be selected quickly. Too much tends to confuse — too little is not effective. For example, in a numerical system of a hundred thousand folders, five digits of color coding will identify a specific folder.

If only one digit was color coded, there would be 10,000 folders with the single digits 0 through 9 color coded. With two digits color coded, there would be 1,000. With three there would be 100 and with four, 10; with five digits color coded, there would be only one folder with the same five digits color coded.

The remaining digits should be printed in black without color coding. The rule is to color code only digits needed to identify and quickly locate the folder. Keep it as simple as possible.

ALPHABETIC COLOR CODING

So far we have discussed the color coding of numeric filing systems. Other types of filing, such as subject, alphabetic, and alpha-numeric, are also in wide use. The observations about the advantages of shelf filing and color coding apply equally to any system. Self-adhesive, color-coded labels are available for the digits, 0 through 9; for the alphabet, A through Z; year and month labels are also available.

In addition, so called "name" labels can be an integral part of a folder labeling system. Name labels may show names, addresses, social security numbers, account names, primary subjects, secondary subjects, tertiary subjects and reference numbers. Best of all, the name label can be made machine readable for total records control by a microprocessor. It is the *flexibility* of folder identification and color coding that makes it useful for *any* system.

CONVERSION TO LATERAL FILING

Sometimes conversion to lateral filing and color coding is a major undertaking because top-tab folders in current use have documents attached with fasteners. Furthermore, the folder in use may be heavy, expensive pressboard, in good condition. Here, use of "attach-a-tabs" facilitates an economical changeover.

Attach-a-tabs are manufactured in a process similar to automatically applied labels, and can be manually attached to the folders in use. Thus, another method is added to ways of achieving efficiency when changing from drawer to color-coded lateral filing.

MYLAR® REINFORCED FOLDERS

Another recent development in end-tab filing systems is the Mylar® reinforced folder. These are made of 14 point folder stock with a double thickness on the ends of front and back panels. Additionally, there is a four-inch-wide strip of Mylar® laminated to the stock, wrapped around the double thick ends, providing reinforcement at the wearing edges.

Mylar® is a superior surface for attaching self-adhesive color-coded labels. This Mylar® reinforcement comes clear and in ten different colors — another element in building flexibility.

TOTAL RECORDS CONTROL

We have examined two major developments in records management that have been gaining strength for several years. The first is a changeover from drawer to lateral or shelf filing with side-tab folders. The second is a series of developments in color coding, each adding more flexibility and usefulness to the folder.

There is a third development that complements the other two and provides total records control.

Here we use the modern wonder tool, the microprocessor. In the last few years, the cost has dropped dramatically and thus, its use in records management is even more profitable.

THE MICROPROCESSOR

Here is how the microprocessor is used to implement total records control.

First, we start with color-coded folders, with a bar code optically readable by a hand-held wand. This is for computer identification of the folder, the same way tomato cans are identified with bar codes in supermarkets. Bar coding makes it easy to enter complex file numbers into the system.

There are two types of machine-readable codes. One is the bar code mentioned above and the other is an OCR code (Optical Character Recognition). Here human-readable numbers and letters are "read" by a hand-held wand.

Next is the database, a record of pertinent information about every folder in the system. With a microprocessor, the same data that is used to automatically manufacture color-coded folders can be loaded in the

Mylar is the registered trademark of Dupont de Nemours.

storage disk of the microprocessor. When this is done, total records control of folders is readily accomplished.

The hardware of the main file control station consists of a CRT, keyboard, hand-held wand, and a report printer. There is also a printer for "request" labels which route folders from the file room to other stations. Such stations have CRTs, keyboards, and wands.

A TYPICAL APPLICATION

Let's assume that we are dealing with the mortgage records of a bank or trust company, and a microprocessor system is in operation.

We have just received an application for a mortgage. It is placed in the next prenumbered, color-coded folder. It is passed to the microprocessor operator who keys into the storage disk: (a) the client's name, (b) mortgage number, and (c) code number of the mortgage officer. Date and time are automatically recorded. A self-adhesive name label is automatically typed and attached to the folder.

ROUTED THROUGH MICROPROCESSOR STATION

The folder is then passed to a mortgage officer who begins the routine for accepting or declining the mortgage. Other personnel may be involved. Each time the folder changes hands, it is routed through the microprocessor control station where the storage disk is updated. In this way, the current status of the application is known at all times.

During approval procedures, various dates are noted on the application including: (a) maturity, (b) renewal, (c) date partial funds advanced, (d) date funds fully advanced, (e) completion of documentation. Each time the folder, with the application, is sent to the microprocessor operator, it is quickly identified by passing the hand-held wand across the machine-readable mortgage number.

The operator records in the storage disk various dates relative to the application. Also, the operator records whether the application was approved or declined. Each time an entry is made, date and time are automatically recorded.

CROSS REFERENCING NAMES AND NUMBERS

With the data for all mortgage applications, in process or approved, on the disk, we can discuss total records control of mortgages. For example, a function of the system is to cross-reference mortgage numbers and clients' names. If someone enquires about a mortgage and

Starting with paragraph A, file folder dealing with an a typical application in the medium-sized bank.

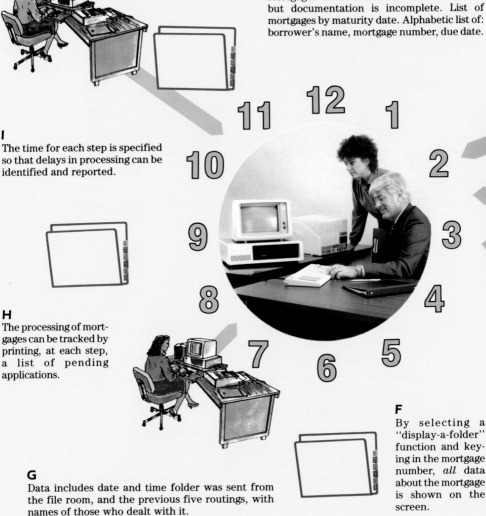

This is an automatic labeler, creating machine-readable folders at high speed. Blank folders are labeled alphabetically or numerically and can also show names.

J

Typical information that can be generated: List of folders charged out to each person. Mortgages where funds have been advanced but documentation is incomplete. List of mortgages by maturity date. Alphabetic list of: borrower's name, mortgage number, due date.

I

The time for each step is specified so that delays in processing can be identified and reported.

H

The processing of mortgages can be tracked by printing, at each step, a list of pending applications.

F

By selecting a "display-a-folder" function and keying in the mortgage number, *all* data about the mortgage is shown on the screen.

G

Data includes date and time folder was sent from the file room, and the previous five routings, with names of those who dealt with it.

APPLICATION

we follow the progress of a
individual mortgage, through
mortgage department of a

At right is a filing hardware "basic"—an installation of movable hanging boxes on steel rails. This affords maximum visibility and accessibility, utilizing the inherent speed, economy and accuracy of color-coded filing.

A
File folders are color coded, with pressure sensitive labels applied with precision.

K
Provision is made for quick recovery of files from dormant storage. The system pinpoints: date, time, number, and file location. Folders can be instantly found.

B
Our folder starts its journey as a new application for a mortgage, is placed in the next pre-numbered, color-coded folder and passed to the microprocessor operator.

C
Operator records applicant's name, mortgage number and loan officer's code number on the computer disk, and the printer makes a label. Date and time are automatically registered.

D
The folder is passed to the loan officer.

E
Going through the approval/rejection cycle, the mortgage application is cross-referenced for mortgage number and borrower's name. When someone needs information about a mortgage, but doesn't know the number, operator keys in first three letters of borrower's name. An alphabetic listing appears on the screen and is "paged up" until the name, with number, appears.

SUMMARY OF CONTROL STATION FUNCTIONS

Besides the file room control station, microprocessor installations typically have as few as four CRT's in user departments to as many as forty or fifty in major companies.

The system's design can include other specific functions for each company's individual needs. Typically, the control station:
•Enters information on new folders into the systems. •Sets up access codes which limit use of system to authorized personnel. •Inquires for, or lists, any and all folders: alphabetic, numeric, and alpha-numeric. •Charges out folders after verifying authorization ... date, time, employee number ... and logs pertinent information into disk memory. •Transfers folders from one user to another. •Keeps track of the last, and the five previous, routings.

25

doesn't know the mortgage number, the operator keys in the first three letters of the client's name. A listing appears on the screen, in alphabetical order, of names starting with those first three letters and is "paged up" until the sought-after name, with number, appears. If a client holds two or more mortgages, the one with the appropriate maturity date is selected.

Next, by selecting the "display-a-folder" function, and keying in the mortgage number, all data about the mortgage is shown on the screen. This includes the name of the person currently using the folder, and the date and time it was received. Also shown would be the five previous routings with names of those who dealt with the mortgage.

CURRENT INFORMATION IMMEDIATELY AVAILABLE

In this way, up-to-date information for any mortgage or application is immediately known, all recorded on the storage disk. The processing of applications can be tracked by printing lists of pending mortgages. Delays in processing can be monitored by specifying the time allowed for each stage.

Here are typical reports that can be generated: (a) Listing of all folders charged out to each person showing date and time folder was sent, (b) All mortgages where documentation has not been completed, even though funds were fully advanced, (c) Listing of mortgages by maturity date or (d) Alphabetical listing showing clients' names and mortgage numbers with due dates.

One of the functions performed is to "reserve-a-folder." This sends it to a user at a future date. Or to "request-a-folder," sending the folder from file room to user. If the folder is "out-of-file," this shows on the CRT screen, in which case the "locate-a-folder" function tells the requester who is using it. Another feature is that only authorized persons can use the system, and only after keying in their personal password.

RECORDS RETENTION SCHEDULE

A problem in any system is to make sure that, as records become inactive, they are moved to dormant storage. Also, if a record is needed from storage, that it can be located quickly. The microprocessor deals with such problems in that lists of folders by category are prepared according to any specified date or time period. Records retention schedules are important because of legal implications and housekeeping requirements. A company should adopt a consistent policy for the length of time various types of records are kept. The microprocessor helps administer that policy.

EASILY ADAPTABLE

It is unusual to make a significant improvement in a system without changing what people do. With a microprocessor, what people do remains much the same, but the manager has, at long last, an effective tool for controlling work. The mortgage records example we have been discussing is typical. Microprocessors are flexible, easily adaptable to meet the requirements of many systems. They are a powerful instrument for exercising total records control.

A CALL FOR ACTION

We have been discussing recent significant developments in records systems. First the changeover from drawer to lateral filing, then the benefits of color coding and, finally, we closed the circle with the microprocessor, leading to total records control.

There are some lucky companies which have, until now, followed the "ostrich" psychology, avoiding problems of the filing mess by hiding their heads in the sand. This is their time of opportunity! Now they can take advantage, in one meaningful action, of the many proven advances in records management available today.

A patch up job, or tinkering, will not produce desired results. What is needed is a fresh start. The better the records system, the more efficient business becomes. In turn, customer service is improved. Good record keeping is the foundation of a well-run business. We should build, as the wise man built, upon such a rock.

THE CORPORATE FILE PLAN

This is why many companies adopt a corporate file plan that encompasses all business records and includes retention schedules. It pulls together recent advances and technological improvements and moves responsibility for administering policies to a higher management level. Also included in the corporate file plan are the filing of computer printouts, floppy disks, and magnetic tapes.

There is a difference between two categories of information — data and documents. Data is usually recorded on the corporate computer system. This information is mostly management statistics, customer databases or financial and business overviews. It defines the *status* needs of the organization.

However, this information relies on documents, regardless of the media used to record them. In many organizations this *document proof* is neglected. It is this hard-copy paper information that we are talking about in this book.

The use of a microprocessor allows all corporate documentation to be identified, indexed, located and moved expediently through the normal records life cycle. Past efforts to do this have often failed because the procedures have been too labor intensive. With microprocessor control of records, intelligent decisions can be made faster, especially when it is known what information is available and exactly where it is.

Efforts to get rid of paper as a media for documents becomes less of a priority as control of the paperwork becomes a reality. In fact, many professionals are rediscovering the advantages of paper.

ADVANTAGES OF PAPER

We should not be so mesmerized by technology as to overlook these advantages. One great virtue is that we avoid the conversion expense and time involved in changing to some other medium. We are used to paper, so why change just for the sake of change?

There is another subtle advantage to paper, involving memory recall. As we read a letter, it is registered in memory. The mind also remembers notations on the letter and a thought process is generated. When we see it a week, month or years later, we somehow recall our thinking. The letter, with its notations, is "image-rich" and mysteriously triggers memory. Our mind is a wonderful instrument. Let's use it to the limit!

For legal admissibility, there is no better evidence than the original document. This requirement is often so important that, regardless of anything else, the paper must be kept. Another advantage is that people do not require training to process paper. Everyone is comfortable with it. Finally, don't overlook the ability of computers to cross-index documents, using key-word indexing, so that fast reference to any document can be part of the system.

PAPER STILL DOMINATES

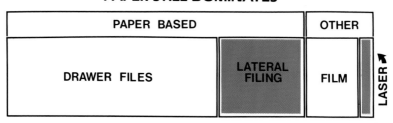

Paper is by far the most popular medium for business record-keeping, especially for active records. New technologies, such as optical disk, and electronic information systems, have their place in very large, special purpose systems.

II
PUTTING NAMES IN ALPHABETIC ORDER

The development of good filing systems for paper-based records requires adherence to a set of rules for putting names in alphabetic order. Unless uniform rules are used, filing documents in file folders where names are on the folder tabs will eventually result in misplaced folders and lost records.

Also, the key to a good *numeric* filing system is a meticulously maintained alphabetic index.

How to do this may seem so obvious that one may wonder why the topic is discussed here. In fact, while most people know in general how names should be arranged for filing or for maintaining an index, there is no agreement on the *details* of how to get the job done! When it comes to making rules for filing, there are many, and they can be so complex that it needs a Philadephia lawyer to figure them out.

ARMA GUIDELINES FOR ALPHABETIC FILING

Two approaches for selecting uniform rules for arranging names alphabetically are discussed here. The first is the ARMA guideline from the Association of Records Managers and Administrators and secondly, a simplified method, following the procedures used in telephone directories. Readers are encouraged to investigate the merits of both approaches. The ARMA guidelines may be purchased from:

> Association of Records Managers and Administrators
> 4200 Somerset Drive, Suite 215
> Prairie Village, Kansas 66208

These rules were developed over a period of thirty years by various committees of ARMA members who are veteran records managers and file management professionals. ARMA is a recognized authority in records management methods.

THE PHONE DIRECTORY RULES

Another way to file alphabetically is to follow the rules of the telephone companies. Their rules are simple, straightforward and easy to follow.

Here they are:

★ Disregard Ampersands (&) and Hyphens (-)

File as if there were two separate words.

Clayton-Powell	becomes	Clayton Powell
Johnson & Johnson	becomes	Johnson Johnson
Jones & Co.	becomes	Jones Co.

★ Disregard Apostrophes (')

In this way, Bob's Shop becomes Bobs Shop.

★ Initials Precede First Names

For example, "Harris, R." comes before "Harris, Albert."

Harris,   A.
Harris,   R.
Harris,   Albert

★ Spell Out Abbreviations

Certain abbreviations, like "St. James Hospital," are listed alphabetically as if spelled out in full: "Saint James Hospital."

Saint Hill
St. James Hospital
Salsbury

★ Numbers Are Spelled Out

Numbers used as names, like "521 Club," are treated as if spelled out in full: "Five Twenty-One Club."

Five Star Club
521 Club
Fix-It Shop

★ Prefixes Are Part of the Name

For example, "Macneil" follows "MacNab."
MacNab
Macneil
MacPherson

★ "The" Follows a Company Name

The Fabric Shop	filed as	Fabric Shop, The
The Jewel Store	filed as	Jewel Store, The
The Jones Co.	filed as	Jones Co., The

★ With Government Listings, The Province, State, City or Town Precede

Florida, The State Of
Jamesville, The Town Of
Ontario, The Province Of
Oswego, The City Of

Whenever there is more than one way to refer to a name, it should be cross-referenced. For example, Graham Spencer (listed under "S" for Spencer, Graham) will be cross-referenced under "G" for Graham Spencer. A good cross-reference or *relative index* solves many problems. And it doesn't need to be on cards or in a computer. Simply place half a folder on the shelf, showing the cross-reference on the label.

These simple rules will save you a lot of grief. Remember, when in doubt between two locations for the same file — choose one and cross-reference the other. Then you can always locate the file quickly.

One simple idea has proved to be a real asset in alphabetic filing. It is so simple that filing supervisors hesitate to use it. Make up a display card showing the alphabet in inch-high letters, from A to Z. It's easy to make — just go to an art supply house and get a sheet of large, press-on letters. Then post the card in a conspicuous place in the file room. It may seem elementary, but it helps.

One final caution. The ongoing usefulness of any filing system depends to a large degree on a capable and interested file manager. This designated czar of filing ensures that file set-up and maintenance rules are strictly enforced. Disciplined consistency is obviously a must, no matter which method you choose.

31

THE LIBRARY APPROACH

The illustration shows clearly why it is better to file on shelves instead of in drawers. Imagine, if you can, what a Public Library would look like if all the books were stored in drawers.

It is this principle of placing books on shelves that has been adapted by records managers to store file folders. It is simple, straightforward and fast.

The added ingredient, that makes it all possible, is the color coding of the folders. This, so to speak, corresponds to titles on books, and enables anyone to select folders from shelves quickly and easily.

So simple — so direct — so obvious!

III

COLOR CODED SYSTEMS

Today, almost everything is color coded. If you order a telephone, you are asked, "What color?" If you buy a ticket to a sporting event, color directs you to sit in the blues, the greens, or the grays. When color is used, they say, "It's color coded." Well, there is color coding and color coding.

The main purpose of color coding is to reduce time spent searching for a folder and returning it to the file after use. Also, the color-coded labels on folders help locate folders on desks and elsewhere in the office.

FILING BY NUMBERS

A filing system using numbers is easiest to deal with. Numeric systems are simple, direct and effective. Everyone knows numbers. There are ten digits, 0 through 9. Anything can be numbered with ten digits, because, with each move to the left, we multiply by ten. Five dollars becomes five hundred dollars with two moves to the left.

We only deal with numbers in numeric series. We start with the lowest number and end with the highest. Sometimes, and with good reason, the filing specialist plays a game. It's called terminal digit filing, middle digit filing, or other names. If you don't know the tricks, the results seem like magic. It all relates to the arrangement of the files — the file numbers don't change. With numeric filing, knowing the arrangement is understanding the system.

SHUFFLING FILES LIKE PLAYING CARDS

Let's begin with an example in re-arranging numbers. In a deck of playing cards there are four suits — clubs, diamonds, hearts and spades — each with thirteen cards — ace, king, queen, jack, ten, nine, and so on.

33

Usually cards are arranged by suit and then by value. If there were a good reason, they could be shuffled and re-arranged with four aces together, four kings together, etc. In terminal digit filing we, so to speak, "shuffle" files and come up with a different arrangement.

Let us approach it in another way. Suppose the files were in a huge pile, all mixed up. We start by sorting them into ten piles beginning with the units position of the file number. We now have ten groups sorted by digits 0 through 9. Then, we take each of the ten groups and sort them a second time by the tens position, into one hundred groups. If we continued by sorting the one hundred groups by the hundreds position of the file number, we have a thousand groups.

If we continue sorting files this way until they are sorted by the last five digits, the file is divided into a possible hundred thousand divisions. The last five digits of the file number, after this sorting operation, will be in a straight numeric sequence. Then, if these last five digits are color coded, the search for a file will be so limited that a single file can be immediately selected.

TERMINAL DIGIT FILING

In large numeric systems, some form of terminal digit filing is almost universal. Originally, the system was developed to meet the needs of insurance underwriters for filing policies. Most underwriters represent a dozen or so companies, with varied types of insurance. Of the forty or fifty policy series, some are more popular and involve more filing activity.

Originally policies were filed first by policy series, and then in numerical order. This caused a traffic jam because all new policies, the most active files, were added at the end of the numeric series. Then someone got a bright idea and rearranged policies by the two terminal digits. The traffic jam was eliminated because new files were distributed among one hundred two-digit sections. All policies were merged into one integrated system.

At that time, four-drawer cabinets were used for most operations. For ease of explanation, let's say there were a hundred cabinets. One was assigned to each of the terminal two-digit groups, 00 through 99. Each of the four drawers in a cabinet was assigned to the secondary terminal digits, 00 to 24, 25 to 49, 50 to 74 and 75 to 99, respectively. Reference to a policy was by the last two digits, and then by the next two.

THE MOST NEEDED DOCUMENT IS OFTEN MISFILED

This simplified file reference, but there remained a problem of misfiles when a policy was misplaced. Misfiled policies could not be located without a complete search. It always seemed that the most urgently needed policy was the one misfiled!

Of course, the best way to deal with misfiles is not to have any. Misfiles can be controlled through good supervision in the file room and a well-trained staff with a low turnover. When these conditions prevail, there are few problems, and misfiles are minimal. To maintain an organization at this standard of excellence is a challenge.

CHANGING FROM DRAWER TO SHELF FILING

The next major development was a changeover from drawer to lateral filing, together with the introduction of color coding or group identification. The objective was to make certain all folders were correctly filed in one of the hundred terminal-digit divisions and to limit the search for a misfile to a hundredth part of the system.

Two methods were developed for doing this. One involves matching bars, illustrated below. Here the side of the folder is divided into eleven equal parts. The parts, beginning at the top, are assigned to the ten digits 0 through 9. The bottom position identifies a repeat. Corresponding to a particular terminal digit, parts are overprinted in black, thus creating two black bars for each terminal digit. If the first digit is smaller than the second, such as 57, the whole band is printed in green and if the second digit is smaller than the first, such as 75, the band is in orange. If a folder is misfiled, the bars won't line up, in either the green or orange sections of the file.

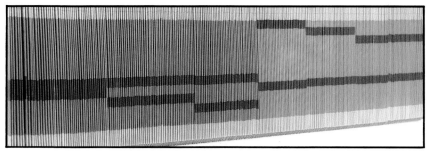

Terminal Digits - using bars

A second method is illustrated below. Colors are assigned to digits 0 through 9. The colors, representing the terminal digits, are printed as two color bands on the edge of the folder. Whenever the color bands for a folder don't match, a misfile is indicated.

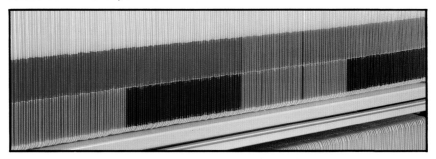

Terminal Digit - using color bands

MISFILES STAND OUT LIKE A SORE THUMB

In both illustrations on this page, we have purposely shown misfiles. Anyone can see how easy it is to find them. Whenever one is discovered it should be corrected immediately. Thus, with every file in its correct group, a search is limited to a specific group. Each segment is about one hundredth part of the filing system.

Sometimes the last three terminal digits are identified with color bands, and files arranged by the last three terminal digits. When this is done the file is divided into a thousand segments. A search for a misfile is limited to about one thousandth part of the filing system.

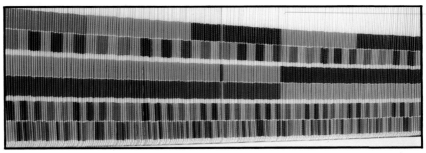

Middle Digit - using color bands

A variation of terminal digit filing is "middle digit" filing, illustrated above. Here, for example, the six-digit file number 27-34-16 would first be filed by the middle digits 34, next by the 27, and lastly by the 16. The advantage of middle digit filing is that when blocks of policies are assigned by a head office to outside agents, these policies, when returned by the agent, are filed together.

With both terminal and middle digit filing, additions are spread throughout the system. This minimizes congestion in the file room, and distributes the work load.

A SUDDEN INCREASE IN EFFICIENCY

Until a few years ago, the color coding of folders served the purpose of insuring that the search for misfiles would be limited to pre-designated groups. For example, all folders with the terminal digit "twenty-five" would be filed together.

Then there was a technical breakthrough in the manufacture of color-coded folders. At little additional cost, the whole file-reference number, or at least five or six digits, could be color coded. But this worked only if the numbers were consecutive. Patient numbers in hospitals, for example, suited this requirement.

There was a tremendous increase in filing efficiency when this was done and, at first, no one could figure out exactly why it happened.

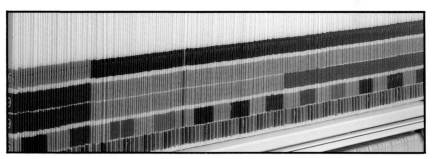

Numeric - using five-digit color coding

The answer seems obvious now. It was because a specific file could be located just by looking at the extreme edge of the folder. The thin lines of color are "read" as numbers. The illustrations on this page show this. Study the colors at the bottom of the page and then "read" the file numbers in the illustration above. After only a few hours, filing people read *colors* instead of *numbers*. Colors are the the new language of filing!

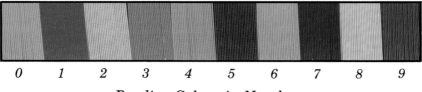

| 0 | 1 | 2 | 3 | 4 | 5 | 6 | 7 | 8 | 9 |

Reading Colors As Numbers

There was another technical breakthrough in the manufacture of color-coded folders. It was the automatic application, under computer control, of single-digit, self-adhesive labels to any type of folder. This automatic labeler enables color-coded folders to be manufactured at machine speed in any sequence. It answers the need, in file conversions, of supplying folders to meet any reasonable filing changeover schedule. A remarkable advance in the art!

FILES EASILY LOCATED — EVEN ON DESKS!

So much for increased efficiency in the file room. It is, however, *outside* the file room that the advantages of fully color-coded filing are most striking. At any one time, for active filing, there may be up to twenty per cent of files circulating in the office. With files fully color-coded, they can be easily located, even when they are in piles on desks.

Bright, easily identified hues and legible numbers and letters of color-coded labels make finding folders fast and simple, even when they are in unorganized piles on desks. Clerk is using a handy rack with three hanging box files.

The person who likes color coding most is the office manager, because it is a powerful management tool. First, if a folder is in the file room, it must be in its allotted place — filed according to the colors on the edge. It cannot be misfiled for long. If it is not in its place in the file, it is just not in the file room. It must be somewhere else, and can be found by a brief search. It's a great feeling to be able to find any file you need in jig time!

SUBJECT FILING

Subject filing does not present any difficulty in the filing operation itself. Once a letter has been read and someone has decided its subject classification, it is easy to put it in the correct folder. But there lies the frustration and difficulty — "What is the subject?" or, "What if there are two subjects?"

This question is answered in two ways. One is by having a private secretary file it according to a secret formula. The other is to establish a "Master Subject Classification Index" that everyone throughout the company understands. Those responsible for maintaining the subject filing system are the people who must thoroughly understand it.

Too many businesses use subject index systems that were established years ago, and do not satisfy today's requirements. This results in an accumulation of poorly classified material. One common fault is to file any letter with a subject not clearly understood under "general."

A TRIP TO A DEPARTMENT STORE

The best subject filing requires, above all else, skilled, capable and experienced people, especially if the files are out of kilter and need revision. One filing specialist explains subject filing by a trip to a department store. If you want wallpaper, you enter the store and ask, "Which department?" You are directed to the Hardware Department on the second floor. (This corresponds to the main subject heading of the master index.) When you get there you are then directed to the Paint Section. (This is a sub-division of the main subject.) You go to the paint section and buy the wallpaper. (Filing people call this the tertiary sub-division.) *So we see that subject filing can be as easy, and as much fun, as buying wallpaper.*

SUBJECT-NUMERIC

Let's not be confused about the name "Subject-Numeric." It is the simple process of assigning numbers to subjects. (The Dewey decimal system is an example.) There are several practical subject-numeric systems. This is because a filing system that is established and works is, de facto, a good one.

In any subject system, color coding can be used effectively to identify subjects, numerics, or a combination of both.

ALPHABETIC FILING

Someone once said that numbers were the working tools of scientists and mathematicians; words and names the tools of writers and poets. Letters lack the precision of numbers and, for filing applications, letters are more difficult to deal with.

What are the chances of a misfile? Take three positions of numbers, 1 2 3 and three letters of the alphabet, A B C. For numbers, we have 10 × 10 × 10 = 1,000 combinations. For letters, we have 26 × 26 × 26 = 17,576 combinations. The mathematics tells us that there are at least ten to fifteen more chances of a misfile when using letters, than when using numbers.

Incidentally, most of us already know about this superiority of numbers and their precision in filing. We all have various identification numbers. They become more important than our names for paying taxes and securing social benefits. Let us hope we never reach that level of efficiency when we will be asked, "What is your number?" instead of "What is your name?" Until that time comes, we will all be dealing with alphabetic filing, probably forever. It is by far the most popular way to file. It is direct and everybody knows how to do it. And what is more to the point, the cross-reference index required when filing by numbers is not needed.

Problems in alphabetic filing relate to the number of files in the system. For smaller systems there is no problem. But with a move to the city, things are different. There are too many Smiths, Joneses and Olsens. And is it William P. or W. Patrick? And is it Smith, Smyth, or Smythe? Is it Olsen or Olson? Even when we know exactly what the name is, and precisely where it should be filed, there is always the chance of a misfile.

First, let's discuss knowing exactly where to file. As the filing operation gets larger, there is a greater necessity for establishing "Rules for Filing." Everyone must know these rules, and the rules must be precise. They deal with such items as: Do we file all the Mac's and Mc's together or file them strictly alphabetically? Do we file under The Keith Burton Co., or Keith Burton Co., or Burton, Keith Co.? Is it The City of Plainfield or Plainfield, The City Of? (See Chapter II for a discussion on alphabetizing.)

PREVENTING MISFILES

There are many answers to that other problem in alphabetical filing — how to prevent misfiles. This really is a question of how to *identify* misfiles. When misfiles are easy to spot, they are easy to correct.

Misfiles relate to the excellence — or lack of it — in file room working conditions, and the files having good guiding and being clearly labeled. Unquestionably, files should not be overcrowded, nor contain outdated or worthless records. Folders must be clearly identified. Good guiding or indexing makes it easy to locate a folder in the file within a few inches. And let's not forget the staff, who should be well-trained, skilled, and interested.

Assuming these considerations have been dealt with, there remains the problem of how to identify a misfile. The solution is to choose a good method of color coding. There are several.

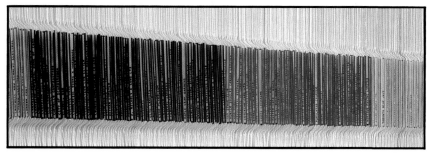

Alphabetic - using color bars

A coding system, using colored file-folder labels, is illustrated above. Here thirteen colors are used twice. Each color identifies a letter in the first half of the alphabet, and a repeat of the color identifies the letter of the last half of the alphabet. Misfiles of the first letter of a name are singled out.

Another method of identifying misfiles is based on the theory that most misfiles are made by the second letter of the name. This assumes that a person can correctly locate the file area of the first letter, and is more likely to misfile by the second letter. In this method, the alphabet is divided into groups by the vowels A, E, I, O and the letter R. These are the five groups: ABCD, EFGH, IJKLMN, OPQ, and RSTUVWXYZ. Each second-letter group is identified by a different colored label. Misfiles are unmatched colors. Identifying the second letter in this way reduces misfiling.

When using file-folder labels with color bars, one must make a decision to use the bars to identify the first or second letter of a name. The identification is made as described above, or by a similar process. Its effectiveness relates to the size of the filing application and the care and attention given its operation.

Illustrated below is the Alpha Binary Code or ABC filing system developed by the Datafile Company. Here twelve colors are used twice, the second time with a distinctive white stripe. Every letter is unique, and cannot be mistaken for another. When the first two letters are color coded, the search for a misfile is limited to a small file section.

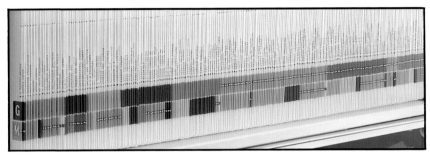

Alphabetic Filing - two letters identified

By color coding two letters of a name, there is a major increase in filing precision, thus limiting the search for a folder. When only one letter is identified, the file is divided into twenty-six segments, one for each letter. But by identifying two letters, the file is divided into three or four hundred segments. (The possible total is 26 x 26 or 676 segments. All combinations of letters do not occur in names.) This increased precision adds another dimension to alphabetic filing.

When this method is used, it is practical to convert numeric filing systems, with up to ten thousand names, to alphabetic systems. This eliminates use of a cross-reference between numbers and names. Reference to names becomes so simple and direct that there are substantial savings in the time the staff takes to locate files.

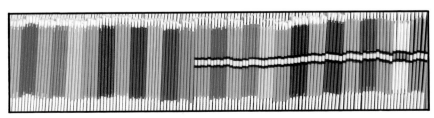

A B C D E F G H I J K L M N O P Q R S T U V W X Y Z

*Since each letter is distinctive –
one letter cannot be mistaken for another*

OTHER USES OF COLOR CODING

Although the main purpose of color coding is to identify a filing series, either alphabetic or numeric, color coding may be used effectively for other purposes.

For example, the month an investment certificate comes into force can be identified with a MONTH LABEL. Then every month, a year or so later, the files for a particular month could be drawn for review with little effort. Or, for example, a YEAR LABEL could be used to identify the year of destruction for expired, lapsed or cancelled policies, at the time they are transferred to inactive storage.

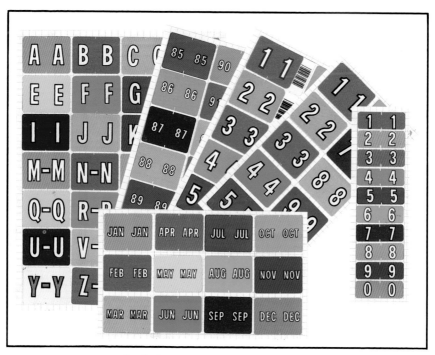

Labels used for color coding

When files are reviewed only once each year, say for transfer to inactive storage, a full year's accumulation of files is dealt with. On the other hand, if they are reviewed every month, there is only a month's accumulation. It's the same as when washing dishes...you accumulate a lot more if you only wash them once a week than you do if you wash them after every meal.

90% MORE
FILING IN THE SAME SPACE

A change in methods results in an ADDITIONAL 4,500 filing inches.

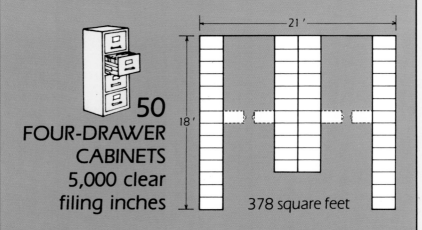

50 FOUR-DRAWER CABINETS
5,000 clear filing inches

378 square feet

34 units of HANGING BOX FILES

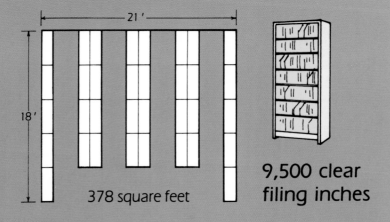

378 square feet

9,500 clear filing inches

IV

FILE LOCATOR NUMBERS

A new way has been found to assign numbers to subjects in subject-numeric filing systems. It greatly simplifies the process. It has many advantages.

The new numbers are called *File Locator Numbers* to distinguish them from the *File Reference Numbers* presently being used in subject-numeric systems.

The new system depends on color coding the folders for each subject, and sub-subject, listed in the Master Classification Index; and on the use of a microprocessor to quickly tell us the file number. Also on the fact that when all digits of the file locator number are color coded, there is only one place on the shelf of folders to find a specific folder. For example, if a folder has the number 25125 it will be located on the shelf between 25124 and 25126. Thus there is one place, and one place only, for folder 25125.

ASSIGNING FILE REFERENCE NUMBERS

First let's review the current procedures for assigning File Reference Numbers. It begins with the Master Classification Index of subjects. The main subjects, called primary subjects, are subdivided into secondary subjects, and then into tertiary subjects. Numbers are assigned to each group. For example, a primary subject could be numbered 125, a secondary 240 and a tertiary 170. Thus we have subject 125-240-170. The underlying idea is to be able to assign reference numbers to subjects in such a way that the numbers will be in the same numeric sequence as the Master Classification Index. In this way the folders on the shelves will be kept in the same alphabetic sequence as the Master Index. This method provides for expansion by adding additional subgroups of numbers, if needed, as new subjects are added.

ASSIGNING FILE LOCATOR NUMBERS

Now let's review another way of numbering the Master Classification Index, using File Locator Numbers. These numbers are in consecutive numeric sequence, and can be numbers of four, five or six digits. Assuming we have a moderately large subject system and will be using a numeric sequence of four digits, then starting at the beginning of the Master Index, we number the first subject 1000 and the next 1001, and the next 1002, etc. until all the subjects are numbered. Suppose we end up with number 3025. The next step is to make up folders corresponding to the assigned File Locator Numbers.

When the next new subject is added it will be number 3026, and the next 3027, etc. In time, the numbers assigned to the subjects will be random in relation to the Master Classification Index.

EASY TO FIND A FOLDER

The best way to operate the system is to use a microprocessor for the Master Classification Index; then the File Locator Number for any subject can be quickly found. Key words can be used to search the index if necessary. A specific subject can be referred to by different names — all pointing to the same File Locator Number. A subject file with some ten thousand subjects need only have a four-digit File Locator Number.

Another alternative is to use a word processor to periodically type out the Master Classification Index for reference in finding File Locator Numbers.

In any case, the folder for a particular subject can be quickly located on the shelf because, with color coding, there is one place and one place only, to find or file the folder.

The file locator system for numbering subjects is simplicity itself. It is remarkably effective, and is another important development in the color coding of filing systems. (See also Personal Files - page 68.)

Think it over!

V

THE MICROPROCESSOR

The heart of the microprocessor is a little silicon chip that is truly the wonder of our age. We have all seen pictures of this quarter-inch square of silicon with its logic circuits. Each chip consists of thousands of transistors and diodes.

Having a microprocessor for filing systems is like having a staff magician who always comes up with the whereabouts of any folder. He is fast — the hand is quicker than the eye. How is it done? That's what we will talk about in this chapter.

The magician spends all afternoon putting a rabbit into a hat so he can pull it out at the right instant. Well, the database of the microcomputer is like the hat. It must be loaded with information about all folders in the system, then programmed to perform all the "functions" we need. *Then* we perform our magic!

Most systems require lots of data, so we need plenty of storage capacity. Computer storage is measured in megabytes or millions of bytes of data. It takes one byte to store a letter or a number. So if one folder record were to require five hundred bytes of data, we would need one megabyte for each two thousand folders (500 x 2000 = 1,000,000). Depending on the number of folders, we will need disk storage capacity of from 20 to 200 megabytes to operate the system.

We also need dynamic memory with its instantaneous response. It usually takes about 512K or 512,000 bytes of this kind of memory. The dynamic memory is used in part for programs that direct functions of the microprocessor, and in part for actually executing the functions. It operates at lightning speed and seeks out the data from the multi-megabyte disk memory only once for each transaction.

Color Coded Folders

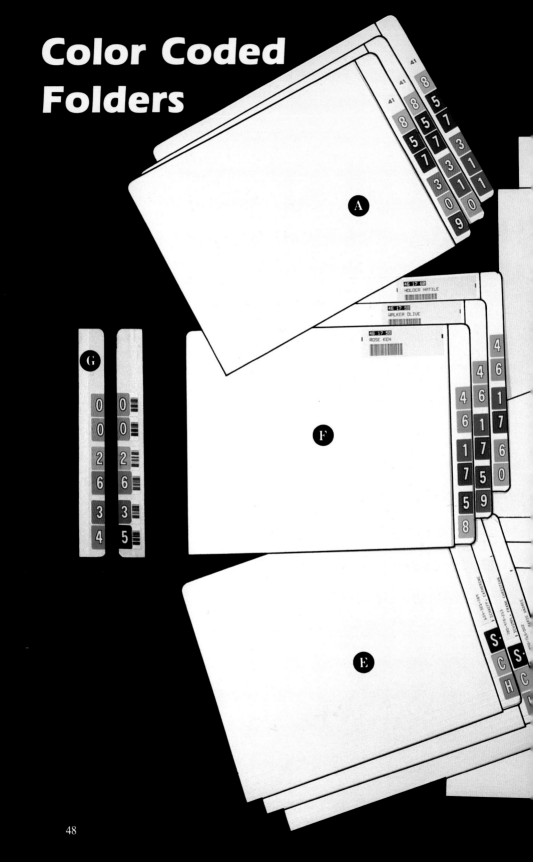

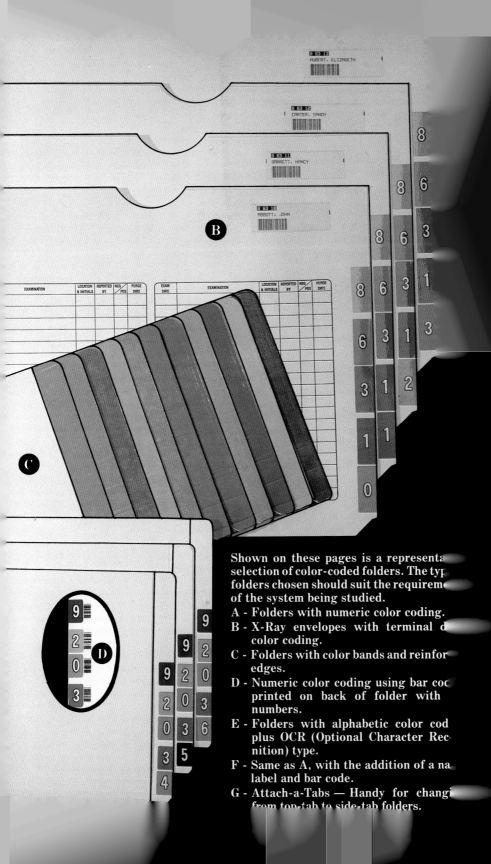

Shown on these pages is a representa[tive] selection of color-coded folders. The typ[e of] folders chosen should suit the requireme[nts] of the system being studied.

A - Folders with numeric color coding.

B - X-Ray envelopes with terminal d[igit] color coding.

C - Folders with color bands and reinfor[ced] edges.

D - Numeric color coding using bar cod[e] printed on back of folder with numbers.

E - Folders with alphabetic color cod[ing] plus OCR (Optional Character Rec[og]nition) type.

F - Same as A, with the addition of a na[me] label and bar code.

G - Attach-a-Tabs — Handy for changi[ng] from top-tab to side-tab folders.

The microprocessor also acts as a traffic cop. It permits only authorized people to use the system and it monitors the flow of data to and from CRTs, printers, keyboards and the wands that "read" folders.

Let's backtrack. Our first requirement is optically readable color-coded folders. If we're lucky, somewhere in the company there will be a data bank containing everything we need, including such items as names, reference numbers, dates of loans or dates of birth; for subject files, the primary, secondary and tertiary descriptions. However we obtain it, the same data used to manufacture color-coded folders is used to load the multi-megabyte storage disk. In addition to data about folders, we need data about users, specifying the particular functions they are authorized to use.

To be effective, we will have file control stations strategically located in areas where folders are used, so that as folders are sent from file room to control areas, they can be "received" for users needing them. Each file station has a CRT with keyboard, and a wand for reading reference numbers on folders. The microprocessor is located in the file room. Connected to it is a printer for reports, and one for "request" labels to route folders to users who need them.

Now, let's assume the system is operational and the database loaded with all needed information about folders, users and functions. The way to know how it works is to understand the functions. These are set out in a menu. Functions are divided into three groups: (a) maintenance, (b) file control, and (c) reports.

For any selected function, the program is self-prompting. The microprocessor won't let you make a mistake. It leads you, step by step, through the process. If you enter non-valid data for a function you select, it will correct you.

MAINTENANCE FUNCTIONS

Maintenance functions make sure the database is always up-to-date. Each function has an abbreviation associated with it. This is called a mnemonic, meaning "to assist the memory." The mnemonic is used to select a function. Here are some examples.

ADF	Add a file
DELF	Delete a file
EDF	Edit a file

These functions are used when folders are added to the system, deleted, or edited for changes.

ADU	Add a user
DELU	Delete a user
EDU	Edit a user

As users change, these functions are used. Each user has access only to specific functions and uses a confidential code word to gain access to the system.

| ASSIGN | Assign a new home |

Each folder is assigned to a particular file room or "home." There can be several file rooms or "homes" for files. This function is used when the "home" is changed.

| LOGON | This gives a user access to the system |
| LOGOFF | Is used when all tasks are completed |

User security codes prevent unauthorized system use. The system keeps track of each user's time on the system.

FILE CONTROL FUNCTIONS

These functions are used for the operation of a typical file control system. As folders circulate throughout the office, their movement is "read" into the system with a hand-held wand by passing it across the optically readable bar or coding.

SEND	Send a file
RECEIVE	Receive a file
TRANSFER	Transfer a file

These are the most commonly used functions. Each time a folder moves from station to station, from person to person, the computer records its new location.

| DSPF | Display a file |
| LOCATE | Locate a file |

The "display" command shows the viewer all data in the system for a particular folder. With the "locate" command, we can identify the current and the previous five users of a folder, and the date and time of each use.

REQUEST   Request a file

A request made for a file from any station will automatically print a routing label in the file room. It will show the time and person requesting the file, and the name and reference number of the file requested. The routing label is attached to the folder.

RESERVE   Reserve a file

When a file is needed at a future date, or is out of the file room, "reserve" will send it to the person requesting it on the day requested, or as soon as it is available.

FFI   Flag for insertion

If a file is out of the file room and correspondence is received, the folder is flagged for insertion of correspondence when the folder is returned.

SEARCH   Search by name

This is a cross-reference. When the first three letters of a name are entered, it will display an alphabetical listing showing the reference numbers corresponding to the names.

REPORT FUNCTIONS

Depending on requirements of a particular application, there are a variety of reports that may be programmed into the system. Typical examples are:

Files in reference number sequence
Files in alphabetical order
Overdue files charged to users
All files in use
All reservations by date
All flagged files for insertion of correspondence
All files not used for a given number of months
All users

File control station, where files are charged out to individuals or departments. Microprocessors bring filing systems into the Twentieth Century.

A VERSATILE MANAGEMENT TOOL

The microprocessor, an amazing control tool, can be programmed to serve the specific needs of an organization. Some of the benefits:

- Location of each folder, in or out of file room, is always known.

- Folders can be requested from the file room from any control station. A "request" label printed in the file room is attached to the folder, and becomes a "routing" label. (This happens only if the requested folder is in the file room.)

- Any folder can be reserved and sent to a user at a future date.

- Folder can be flagged for insertion of correspondence received when it is out of file room.

- If folders are kept by a user longer than an approved length of time, an "overdue" list can be printed.

- Only authorized users can operate the system.

- Folders are assigned to a "home" file room. Different groups may have different "homes." When folders are transferred from active to dormant storage, the "home" is changed.

- Policies are established for transfer of files from active to dormant, based on activity or length of time from the last reference. Lists of such folders are prepared.

- Retention schedules for folders in dormant storage are maintained. When the retention period ends, lists of folders to be destroyed are produced.

- Names and numbers are cross-referenced. Folders or groups of folders can be printed by name or reference number.

The microprocessor's ability to cross-reference file classification descriptions makes it extremely useful in subject filing. The master index classifies subjects by primary, secondary and tertiary description. Sometimes subjects are called by different names. They can also be referred to by specific "key words." These complexities of cross-referencing are easily dealt with by the microprocessor.

We are learning new ways to use microprocessors to control filing systems. But each system is different from every other. Since there are no standard problems, there are no standard answers. However, the microprocessor is adaptable to most problems when we define the needs of a particular system and select the best solution.

VI

THE FILING SURVEY

The subject of improving records systems deserves management's attention, because office productivity relates directly to the efficiency of the filing operation. This is especially true today, when paperwork is on an upward spiral in both volume and complexity. An important transaction may come to a full stop if a needed folder cannot be found.

An essential for improving the records system is to conduct a survey. Here we discover all the facts relating to a particular system. We do this to analyze, study and devise improvements. But we should not make changes just for the sake of change. There should be measurable dollar savings, increased efficiency and improved control.

A good idea, when starting the filing survey, is to get an understanding of what might be called "the big picture." This is sometimes called "the walk-through." The idea is to become alerted to obvious problems such as lost or misplaced files, and to opportunities for improvements such as better service and lower costs. When doing this you get to know the people involved. Remember to keep them informed about what you are doing and the purpose of the survey. The people doing the work from day-to-day know most of the answers. The trick is to gain their confidence. This is a two-way street and, above all, we must justify their confidence in us. It is important not to make premature judgements — don't jump to conclusions about solutions. Keep an open mind.

BAR CHART SHOWS COST SAVINGS

Let's look at the bar chart on the next page to understand where there is the greatest potential for savings. The chart shows average costs for each $100.00 spent, and compares costs of drawer filing, shelf filing, and shelf filing using color coding. The elements with greatest savings potential are space and clerical cost.

When we save 40% of space by using shelf instead of drawer filing, we reduce space cost from $11.70 to $7.10, thus saving $4.60 out of every $100.00 spent. Even larger savings are available in clerical costs. A reduction of 25% by using lateral instead of drawer filing saves $13.80 and, using color coding, $25.40. Many case examples confirm that such savings are quite common. (For instance, see page 44.) However, every system must stand on its own feet. That is why we need the facts from a filing survey.

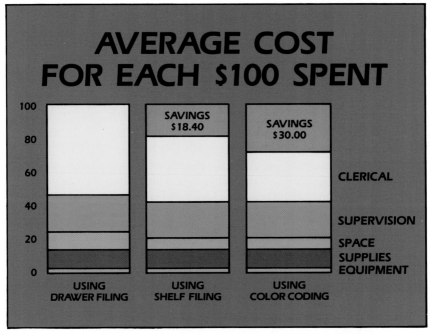

Average savings with shelf filing and color coding.

SHELF FILING AND COLOR-CODED FOLDERS

There are two basic reasons for space savings. First, the aisles between cabinets are reduced because no space is needed for pulling out drawers; and second, because files go higher. The additional height is readily usable since files are accessed from the side, using side-tab folders, instead of over the tops of drawers. Space savings can easily be determined by comparing floor layouts of present drawer filing with proposed shelf filing. Often, when there is just no more room, additional *space* or space *savings* must be found. An answer to the problem is to change from drawer to shelf files. At that time, we should consider changing folders to side tab with color coding.

Clerical cost savings relate to the ability to access files directly. It is like selecting a book at a library where books are always visible on shelves. It is easy to choose the one you want. Just imagine, if you can, a library where books are hidden in drawers. (See page 32.)

VISIBILITY AND LOCATION SENSE

When all folders are visible, a location sense develops. As you approach the files, you start moving towards the one you want. Good visible guide or index systems lead you to the right section. With color coding, especially in numeric systems, you quickly locate the folder you want. There is a double advantage when folders are returned to the file. Here the same file location sense applies. The more active the folders, the greater the savings. *Again, case examples consistently confirm that color coding makes worthwhile savings in clerical costs.*

There is an often overlooked advantage in color coding. It is being able to quickly locate folders that are out of file, on desks, somewhere in the office. You just look at the folder edges to find the one you want.

There is an additional advantage to optically readable color-coded folders. It opens the way for using a microprocessor to provide the ultimate in folder management.

BEGINNING THE SURVEY

So far we have talked about the objectives of the filing survey to achieve measurable dollar savings, increase efficiency and improve control. But how is it done? There is no easy answer. The first step is to take an inventory of the filing. Illustrated, on page 59, are typical forms used for this purpose. Take a tape measure and start at drawer one, cabinet one. Measure the inches of filing in every drawer. Remember the common denominator for measuring filing is "filing inches." So, for the survey, it does not matter if folders are stored in drawers or on shelves.

Make notations of the kinds and types of records. Are folders overstuffed? How current is the material? How is it referenced? Is each digit of the number significant? Are folders in numerical sequence? Terminal digit order? Alphabetic? By subject? Are files decentralized? If so, a separate inventory should be made for each location.

ANALYZING THE DETAILS

It is during the filing inventory that our thought processes go to work. Consider the folder itself. Is it too light? Too heavy? Are fasteners used? If so, are they really needed? Is there printing on the folder, and does it serve a useful purpose? If legal-size folders are used, would letter-size be adequate? If folders are too thick, could they be divided into volumes? *Question everything.* Take nothing for granted.

The real opportunity in inventory taking is to ferret out problems and discover solutions. As we think about improvements we have made in other systems, we become aware that there are many alternatives to consider. But whether or not we adopt them depends on their cost effectiveness. The inventory of filing is the starting point.

PREPARE A RECORDS SUMMARY

The next step is to prepare a summary of the records. A typical form for this is illustrated. This provides totals for each classification.

The best way to count folders is by sampling. Select a number of drawers at random, count the folders, and divide by the number of filing inches used in each drawer selected. This gives the average number of folders per filing inch. If you multiply by twelve, the result is folders per foot. Make sure the count seems reasonable. Curiously, it is often difficult to be sure of the total number of folders in a system — an important figure! *Make it as accurate as possible.*

THE RULE OF "THIRDS"

Folder totals should be modified in two ways. Growth can affect the totals. We need to look ahead a year or two and estimate how many folders we will have then. Maybe a 20% to 25% annual growth factor should be included. Also, if folders are jammed into drawers or shelves, they are difficult to work with. Leave ample space. On the other hand, we must remember the "one third" rule. It states that *if filing has been neglected, it should be possible to scrap a third of the contents, move a third of the folders to dormant storage, and keep only one third in the active filing area.*

At the outset of our survey we make, to scale, a floor plan showing filing space involved. Measure the room. Then, using graph paper, position files and desks. Later, another layout will be made showing the proposed plan. When this is done, space savings can be calculated and work flow considered. (Refer to page 44 for an example of space savings.)

RECORDS SUMMARY

COMPANY __HENRY SMITH AND CO.__

DEPT. __CENTRAL RECORDS__

DATE __JULY 21 / -__

DESCRIPTION OF RECORDS	FILING CAPACITIES			FOLDERS AND GUIDES		
	NUMBER OF DRAWER	CAPACITY FILING INCHES	IN USE FILING INCHES	NUMBER OF FOLDERS	NUMBER OF GUIDES	REMARKS
CORRESPONDENCE	8	200	131	525	75	FULL TOP TAB 11pt letter
SUPPLIER	16	400	288	722	120	RIGHT TOP TAB 14pt legal
CUSTOMER DOCKET	72	1800	1640	4750	350	1/3 CUT 11pt letter
ACCTS. PAYABLE	20	500	370	1900	-	TOP TAB 11pt letter
	116	2900	2429			
	(29-4 DRAWER FILE)					

RECORDS INVENTORY

COMPANY __HENRY SMITH AND CO.__

DEPT. __CENTRAL RECORDS__

DATE __JULY 21 / -__

CABINET #	DRAWER #	INCHES IN USE	FOLDER SPECIFICATION	TYPE OF RECORD
1 LEGAL	1	16	CORRESPONDENCE ALPHA	FULL TOP TAB 11pt.
	2	19		
	3	22	✓	✓
	4	SPARE	✓	✓
2 LEGAL	5	19	✓	✓
	6	25		TEA POT
	7	16	✓	✓
	8	14/131	✓	✓
3 LEGAL	9	24	✓	✓
	10	24	SUPPLIERS ALPHA	RIGHT TOP TAB 14 pt.
	11	17	✓	✓
	12	14	✓	✓
4 LEGAL	13	22	✓	✓
	14	19	✓ 73 FOLDERS	✓
	15	18	✓	✓ PRESSBOARD 16 GUIDES
	16	21	✓	✓
5 LEGAL	17	17	72 FOLDERS	✓
	18	16	✓	✓ 14 GUIDES
	19	22	✓	✓
	20	SPARE	✓	✓
6 LEGAL	21	16	✓	✓
	22	15	✓	✓
	23	18	✓	✓
	24	25/288	57 FOLDERS	✓
			✓	✓ 18 GUIDES
				✓

Typical forms used to organize information for a useful records summary and inventory.

The next step is to track folders to the people who use them. Look for problems and opportunities for improvement. Talk to users. Observe whether folders are hoarded by users to avoid delays in getting them from the file room.

TARGETING COST SAVINGS

Now comes the difficult part — where judgment and experience count. *This is where we specify a proposed records system designed to produce dollar savings, increased efficiency, and improved control.*

The target elements of cost savings are space and clerical. They will come primarily from the adoption of shelf filing and color coding. And in large systems, from color coding that is optically readable for control by a microprocessor. However, intangible advantages are also important. It is difficult to place a dollar value on increased service to users of folders, better service to customers, and better management control. These benefits can be even more significant than dollar savings.

A CLEAR, CONCISE REPORT

Now comes our assessment, findings, and report on the filing survey. Here we talk about cost effectiveness, or what is called "cost-benefit analysis." The report should include:

- A summary of the present records system and a description of the proposed system, including sample folders and room layouts.

- A listing of advantages and disadvantages of proposed systems.

- A comparison of costs of the present and the proposed systems.

- An unqualified recommendation, based on our findings, to move ahead with the change. This creates an opportunity and places the responsibility on us to make it work.

Let's not forget the people who do the work. They must be brought into the picture before we start. Everyone should be shown that the change is a good one, and also be told what part they will play. Regardless of how close to perfection the system may be, its successful operation depends on the dedication and enthusiasm of those who operate it. Their help is essential. Office productivity relates directly to the efficiency of the filing system.

VII
THE EVOLUTION OF
RECORDS MANAGEMENT

For years, the traditional way to file papers was in a folder in a four-drawer cabinet. As you might expect, management went along with the tradition. The answer to almost any filing problem was to get another cabinet or another clerk. It was the cheap and easy answer. But not any more.

Today, there is a new, exciting world of filing systems, with many options. It's a challenging world. A good system can do many things. It increases the productivity of a whole office, not just the file room. It virtually eliminates the cost and inconvenience of lost files. It assists in providing better customer service. Best of all, it saves lots of money!

SOLVING THE PROBLEM

The root of the problem is that many systems started small and just grew. When a system is small, nothing much matters. But as it grows, problems grow faster than filing. Floor space becomes a major issue. This is especially true when less active files are not removed. Often the only reason changes are considered is because there is no more room. Also, space is analyzed when offices are moved to new premises. Then the reality of cost per square foot inspires deep thinking.

An easy way to save space is to take filing out of drawers and put it on shelves. While this saves space, it can aggravate other problems, and even create some of its own. It is necessary that folders be changed from top to end tab.

One question that must be answered is: "Can the expense of changing folders be justified?" The answer can only be found through a filing survey, plus a cost-benefit analysis.

The records survey should be broad enough to take in the file room and the entire records management system. It should start when documents are created, tracing them through all processes, until they are eventually destroyed. The best starting point for the survey is the file folder. We should look at its physical characteristics and labeling, as well as its contents.

An efficient folder is the basic unit of a good system. Using the right folder pays off handsomely. We start from the premise that it can be:

- filed and found quickly
- designed to eliminate misfiles
- located easily, wherever it is
- requested from file room and speedily dispatched to the user
- cross-indexed between numbers, names or subjects
- identified when it becomes inactive
- disposed of when no longer useful

Such a folder helps answer these questions: How much better can the system serve our people? How can productivity be increased? How can it improve service to customers? How much money can we save?

CHANGES IN RECORDS MANAGEMENT

Let's step back, gain perspective, and briefly review developments in recent years. Number one, we are no longer dealing with filing, but with records management — the whole sphere of information that serves our organization. Filing systems play a key role. In this book, we consider only paper processing. We must deal with it because it will be with us for a long time. We now have all the tools needed to deal effectively with paper. Our challenge is to make the best use of them.

Improvements have come about slowly, in stages. They overlap and often depend on the evolution of specialized manufacturing equipment. Most were developed in response to a perceived need. The paradox is that, unless a product is available to satisfy the need, little can be done.

Today we have equipment that will satisfy our filing system needs. We have to match the right products with specific needs. We can do this only after determining what those needs are. This takes imagination, because the requirements of every filing system are different. There is no standard problem, so there is no standard solution.

THREE MAJOR IMPROVEMENTS

Over the years, there have been three major improvements in records management. First was saving space, using various kinds of filing equipment. Next, a number of advances were made in better visual identification by color coding. Although there are many methods of color coding, there is a best way for each application. Finally, we come to the control of all records activity by the microprocessor.

FROM FOUR-DRAWER CABINETS TO SHELVES

First, let's look at space savings. The big step forward took folders out of four-drawer cabinets and put them on shelves, where they are filed higher than in drawers. Shelf filing requires less aisle space.

Sometimes a compromise is made at this step and folders are put in roll-out cabinets. Here drawers pull out sidewise instead of back to front. The advantage is that folders don't have to be changed from top to end tab. It is a marginal improvement, hardly worth the trouble.

CHANGE FOLDERS TO END TAB

When adopting fixed shelf filing, folders should be changed from top tab to end tab. With shelf filing, there are no drawers to pull out or push in. To get the folder, you reach up to the side of the folder instead of going over the top of a drawer. There is usually a forty-percent savings in space. It is a worthwhile gain in space, convenience and efficiency.

CABINETS OR OPEN FILING?

There are several choices in types of shelf filing. There are cabinets with fixed shelves using file supports to hold folders upright. Those in general use are six-high with retractable doors that recess under the shelves. Doors can be gang locked. For greater flexibility and economy there is the open type with plastic boxes that hang from rails. Seven or eight levels can be reached. This is the best answer if records do not have to be locked up, or are all in a secure room.

For slower moving, less active folders, there is mobile filing. Here several banks of files can be moved, manually or automatically, so that only one aisle is used, selectively, to gain access. The space savings are substantial. As you might expect, this equipment is expensive.

As mentioned above, when changing from drawer to shelf filing, folders should be changed from top to end tab. Since ends of all folders are visible, we are naturally led to the consideration of color coding.

MANUFACTURE COLOR-CODED FOLDERS IN ADVANCE

A factor that dramatically simplifies filing changeovers is that end-tab color-coded folders can be manufactured in advance *by using automatic labeling equipment directed by a microprocessor.* Input to the microprocessor can be either from a magnetic tape, or by manually creating a data tape in advance.

There is unlimited flexibility in the format of color-coding. It may be alphabetic, numeric, or a combination. Identification may include the name of a person, full reference numbers, and descriptions of subjects. Reference numbers may be sequential or random. In other words, visual identification of the folder is tailor-made to fit requirements of any application.

THE ENGINE OF PROGRESS

This complete flexibility in preparing color-coded systems in advance is the engine of progress for effective records management. It's the key factor for successfully dealing with paper. Best of all, folders can be made optically scannable (with bar codes or OCR). When this is done, microprocessors can control movement of folders throughout the office.

There are several ways to color code folders. For example, folders in use may be costly to replace because they are made of pressboard with papers attached by fasteners. Here, use of an "attach-a-tab" may be the answer. This is a reinforced, fully color-coded self-adhesive strip or label. It can be attached to folders in use, changing them from top to end tab. Similar strips can be used for re-labeling X-ray jackets in Radiology Departments of clinics and hospitals.

Why is the subject of color coding confusing? It is because, over the years, many variations have developed. Most resulted from the inability of manufacturers to supply what was really needed.

For example, when only the two terminal digits of a number are color coded, the system has limited utility. In a system with a hundred thousand folders, there would be a thousand folders with the same two terminal digits. There is only moderate usefulness in such coding.

The best color-coded system is a balance between too little and too much. Too much is confusing and expensive; too little, of limited use. We should remember that *the primary objective of folder labeling is to locate the folder quickly.*

Keep it simple!

THE MICROPROCESSOR — WAVE OF THE FUTURE

We now come to the most significant development in records control for large systems. This is the elusive piece needed to complete the jigsaw puzzle in our search for better records management. It is the wave of the future — the microprocessor. It serves best when used to complement and enhance a good color-coded system.

Using a microprocessor is more and more attractive because costs are becoming dramatically lower and computer power dramatically greater. With color-coded folders that are optically scannable, we achieve our objectives of making the system better serve our people, increasing productivity, serving customers better, and saving money.

TEAMWORK DOES IT!

But of course, it all depends on the quality of our filing survey and cost-benefit analysis.

A basic suggestion – we should keep up with the state of the art. The best way is to make friends with people who have records management installations that work well. Visit with them. Talk with people in the records management business whom you respect. There are always leaders, and we should follow their lead.

Make a complete survey of the system under study. Measure filing space. Take sample counts of activity. Prepare a cost-benefit analysis.

When changing systems, everyone should be involved. They should be informed through discussions, and a well thought out indoctrination program. Questions should be anticipated and answered in advance. We have been talking about tools. The most important element is the people who use the system. It is people who do things, and management that gives people support and encouragement. Teamwork does it!

EFFECTIVE FILING

From blank folders to microprocessor-controlled systems...
sophisticated color coding forms the basis for the most
cost-effective modern filing.

2
Labels can be in any format,
usually machine readable.
Folders are systematically
arranged in lateral filing
equipment.

1
We begin with blank folders,
speedily identified by the
computer-operated labeler,
with color coding (2).

3
See Chapter III for photos of
a variety of color coding.

6
The records manager, aided
by total records control,
knows (or can find out at any
given time) the exact location of every folder in his or
her department.

4
Files, at one of several control stations, in a typical
microprocessor-directed filing installation, with printer
and with tracking speeded
by hand-held wand (5).

5
Data entry clerk with wand
reads thick and thin bar-
coded indices on labels.

PERSONAL FILES

Thanks to modern color coding and microprocessor technology, a fresh look can be taken at a simple alphabetic-numeric indexing method for personal files.

The key to this method is an alphabetic list of all subjects. When a new subject is received, it is inserted into the list at its appropriate alphabetic location. A supply of color-coded file folders is labeled numerically, for example, 101, 102, 103, 104, 105, ... etc. There are no gaps in the numeric series, and it may continue as far as necessary to accommodate all files. Subjects are placed in the pre-numbered folders, starting with the first folder number. The number is recorded opposite the subject name on the alphabetic list.

The integrity of the alphabetic directory is maintained, as noted above, by inserting each subject in its appropriate place. The integrity of the numeric sequence is preserved because it is never disturbed. It begins as a complete, consecutive number series and stays that way. The alphabetic-numeric cross-reference list is the connecting link that makes the system work.

Modern color coding methods and microprocessor technology make the alphabetic-numeric approach to subject filing worth considering.

First, moving files from drawers to shelves makes them more accessible, and more files can be housed in the same floor space.

Second, by using file folder end-tab labels, and by labeling folders with easily-read color-coded numerals, the accuracy and efficiency of locating and putting files away are greatly improved.

Third, by keeping the alphabetic-numeric cross-reference list on a microprocessor we acquire the power and flexibility necessary to make this system work. New subjects are entered in their exact alphabetical sequence, and the next available numerically pre-labeled folder is automatically assigned to it. If a microprocessor is not available, a listing of the subjects can serve the same purpose.

The alphabetic-numeric approach also solves a chronic subject filing problem. Many subjects have more than one name. But when the folder is filed, it must be put in only one place. With the alphabetic-numeric system, one subject can be identified with several different names, all of which point to the same folder number.

VIII

THE IMPORTANCE OF PEOPLE

It's beyond the scope of this little book to do more than scratch the surface of the very large topic of human behavior. However, we may succeed in suggesting several useful starting points; a few examples will serve to illustrate the importance of people in filing.

A consultant friend relates an experience that demonstrates the theme of this chapter. He and his client, a records manager, were engrossed in a systems problem when her telephone rang.

She answered promptly, "Records. May I help you?" and listened for a moment. "You'll have to excuse me," she said. "One of my people has been hurt, and I must go see her."

The accident was not serious, and in a few minutes the manager returned. "Everything's OK, " she said. "Now, where were we?"

"CARING" SCORES A BULL'S-EYE

This simple expression of genuine care scored a bull's-eye. The manager's action let the employee know that, at least in her boss's eyes, she was important.

Another manager we know, in a large government installation, faced the monumental and seemingly hopeless task of developing a sense of self-worth in a demoralized group of fifty filing clerks.

She had all the technical ingredients for success. New shelf filing equipment to replace a sea of four-drawer files. Three hundred thousand end-tab folders, freshly color coded, to replace mountains of dog-eared, indistinguishable folders. A spanking new computerized file-tracking system with every folder identified in its ample data base. She even had the full support of upper management. But without motivated, enthusiastic workers, this manager knew she was licked.

In those dark days, it did look as if she was stymied. Grubby T-shirts and jeans, poor personal presentation, and an atmosphere thick with smoke, were outer signs of discouragement born of years of complaints from users griping about lost files, misfiles and long waits for files.

RECORDS MANAGER WAS NO PUSHOVER

But this manager was no quitter. She saw a way, took it, and stuck to her guns.

What she told her people could be paraphrased like this: "It's been tough. It's still going to be tough for a while, because we've got a conversion to go through. But with the new system, if we all play our part, there's light at the end of the tunnel. And to make sure the system works, I'm appointing the best experts we have to serve on the implementation review committee. *You!*"

By including her staff in this body that could approve or veto each step in the implementation process, the manager showed respect for her people and their role in the new system. Their natural response was to behave so as to earn that respect. Grubby t-shirts and jeans soon gave way to apparel that mirrored an improved self-image.

Thanks to that positive staff motivation the system worked, and continues to work. More than half the staff have been redeployed to interesting new jobs, thanks to a dramatic increase in file room efficiency. The combination of an improved system and a motivated staff have proven the point most emphatically! The users have stopped complaining, and now sing a happy tune.

THE THREE KEYS TO MOTIVATION

A sense of being included, the opportunity to have their input heard and their experience made to count — these are keys to employee motivation. The anecdotes illustrate sure ways of cultivating a meaningful relationship with those who do the work — the file clerks. They are an important part of the team in any successful records management installation.

These simple stories feature two of the three elements that make an effective filing system — the file clerks and the records manager. There is a third important element. Each element is vitally essential, like the legs of a three-legged stool.

The first leg of the stool is the file clerks. They are the people who perform the vital task of filling requests for file folders, keeping them in order and under control, and putting them in the right place when they return to the file room. Sounds simple, doesn't it? Well, the simplest, most theoretically sound system in the world is ultimately only as good as the people who make it work. The right people can make even a poor system look good. Conversely, no system is good enough to survive the abuse of an indifferent staff.

The second leg is the records manager, who is many things to many people. One requirement stands out, as these examples show: a capacity for spontaneous creative action — the positive initiative that stimulates response in kind. When employees know they are considered important, they gladly do their part to live up to their manager's expectations.

MULTI-FACETED MANAGER

The records manager should be resourceful, fair, flexible, cool under fire; above all, a caring human being who unhesitatingly shares credit for the department's success; and whose protective shoulders are broad enough to take criticism when it comes.

The third leg will come as no surprise to anyone conversant with organizational dynamics. Unfortunately, although those who make up this group are easy to identify, they are sometimes difficult to pin down when it comes time to deliver the goods, because the third key player is the user, the one without whom there would be no system. Much attention is given in systems work to defining user requirements — what the system is supposed to do. Looking at it from a different perspective, there is another kind of user requirement — what the *user* is supposed to do. And this can be summed up in the phrase, *"Help to make it work."*

By whatever means it is achieved, this requirement is as vital as any other. If the user fails to help make it work, for all intents and purposes there is no system. It is that simple, and the user is that important. Not surprisingly, the user who participates when the system is being planned is most likely to make it work when it is implemented.

The top of the stool is the seat of power — upper management. How high up? High enough to encompass and support both the records management department and those who use its services. It is a given that, without the understanding support of a management that is interested in making the right things happen, nothing will happen.

The point we are emphasizing is that each leg of the stool, and the seat, are necessary if the system is to work effectively.

BON VOYAGE!

To use another analogy, each of the key players must participate if a records management system is to work — file room staff, the records manager, the system user and management. These four can be likened to the four wheels of a car. Each must be functional if the car is to go.

Let's carry the vehicle analogy a step further. Who drives the car? It is the system designer who can see filing system needs within the context of the management of all business information. The designer guides the selection of the right solution to a particular situation, and works with each of the four participants to deliver the goods.

One final word on this important topic. Maybe it seems that it is too much to ask for all four — motivated staff, competent records manager, users who make it work and an involved management. Maybe you are asking if it would be safe to go with, say, three of the four in place. Well, would you go for a drive in a car with one wheel missing?

The story of filing systems is a story of people. An atmosphere of trust, respect and good humor that includes all of the players is a vital prerequisite for a system that truly works. It is not possible to overemphasize the importance of people in filing!

LIFE CYCLE OF A RECORD

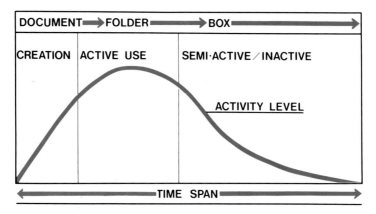

This graph depicts the life cycle of a record, from 'creation to cremation'. It emphasizes, through the curve of the activity line, that the critical time for security, control and efficiency in records management is during the phase when a record is most active.

APPENDIX A
VARIOUS TYPES OF FILES

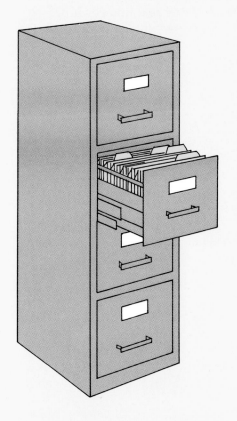

CONVENTIONAL DRAWER FILE

This is the classic file, sometimes called the "Victorian." For many years it was *the* major container of records. Now it is a standard of measure in calculating space savings and efficiency for other types of filing. Hanging pockets in a frame are sometimes added. Folders will stay upright in the pockets without the usual compressor.

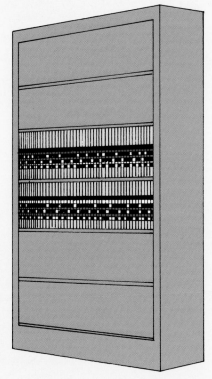

FIXED SHELF (or Lateral) FILE

Many companies have justified the cost of changing from "Victorian" files to fixed shelf cabinets for active filing — especially in large installations. This mode combines space savings with increased efficiency, but necessitates switching from top to side tab folders. Good color coding makes this system dramatically effective. Recessing doors double as work shelves. The cabinets can be locked.

HANGING BOX FILE

For side-tab color-coded files, hanging boxes are the most flexible. Systems are easily expanded, contracted, moved or rearranged. With color coding, this style leads directly to faster filing and finding. It can be tailored to fit dimensions of any room. The open visibility and accessibility speed operations and enhance accuracy. Economy is an important feature of the hanging box filing system.

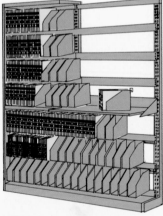

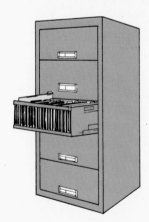

LATERAL (or Rollout or Broadside)

With lateral files, drawers pull out side-ways instead of back to front. Top-tab folders are used. Drawers can accommodate hanging pockets. All folders in a drawer are readily available. There are two variations: drawers with fixed fronts, and pull-out shelves with recessing doors. One drawback — color coding is not very effective with this style.

HANGING POCKET FILE

The slogan of hanging pocket file devotees is that "Every Folder Has a Home." When it's out, and it comes back, there's always a specific place to put it. Pockets are labeled the same as the folders. An empty pocket tells users that the file is out. Correspondence received when the file is out is placed in the pocket and united with the folder when the latter is returned. Though not especially economical of space, or dollars, this method is very satisfactory whenever having a "home" for every folder is paramount.

DOUBLE DEPTH MOVABLE

When cabinets with casters are placed before a bank of like cabinets, important space savings are accomplished. A solid, level base is essential. Less active folders are placed in the back row. This is not for a super-active department, where constant pushing and pulling mobile cabinets could become tedious.

MOBILE FILE

Maximum space is saved when a whole bank of files is placed on a moveable carriage, which runs on tracks. Short banks are operated by hand lever; longer, heavier ones automatically by electric power. Tracks are solidly mounted on a level base. Floor loading specified for the building is not to be exceeded. Since access is limited to one opening in the banks of files, a careful study of activity should be made before committing to this system. It's not for maximum activity offices.

ROTARY FILE

The picture tells it all. Files are on shelves that rotate on a conveyor. The desired shelf is automatically brought to the operator, who can rapidly select or refile any folder in the system. Since there is only one operator per vertical conveyor, this is not recommended for hyper-active file rooms. Naturally, color coding makes this system easier and faster. By using small lights positioned along the shelf edge, a properly programmed computer can select the right shelf and indicate the position of desired folder on that shelf.

TIMES-TWO

It is hard to understand how it works until you have seen it. Fixed shelves, twenty-four inches wide, are back to back. They rotate in a thirty-six inch circle. When rotated, back files become front files. If rotated half way, sides of the shelf ends become the front, thereby closing the file. An ingenious device — well suited to smaller offices.

HORIZONTAL CONVEYOR

File or find a folder without walking. This unit brings a two-foot section of folders right to the operator. Files rotate either forward or backward, and when the right section comes in front of the operator, it stops. If electricity fails, operator can walk to the wanted folder.

TRANSFER DRAWER FILE

This inexpensive drawer file is for storing less active files. Banks of drawers can go ten high. Economical of space and money, drawers store top-tab folders transferred from active files.

TRANSFER BOXES ON SHELVING

Cardboard containers on steel shelving are a standard in record storage centers. Boxes and shelves are designed for compact, waste-free, dormant

filing. Boxes and bays are assigned numbers which, together with a list of box contents, are recorded, usually in a computer base. Thus, specific folders are quickly located and box contents readily scheduled for destruction.

APPENDIX B
VARIOUS TYPES OF FOLDERS AND GUIDES

File folders are manufactured by converting wood pulp chips into a strong paper stock or board. The pulp, naturally dark brown, can be bleached to ivory, beige, pearl white, or the popular "egg shell."

Two factors govern the strength of folder stock. First, the gauge (thickness) of the paper. Folders are usually either 11 point or 14 point. A point is one-thousandth of an inch. The second factor is basis weight — the weight of a specific number of standard size sheets. This figure indicates how tightly the wood fibers are squeezed together. Heavier paper stock, called "pressboard," typically 25 points thick, is made for exceptionally rugged use and is suitable for large capacity expansion folders.

The height of most folders is about 9½ inches. Width varies according to use, i.e. letter, legal or metric. The wearing edge can be folded over on itself, thus becoming reinforced. To provide a superior folder, Mylar® can be wrapped around the reinforced double edge.

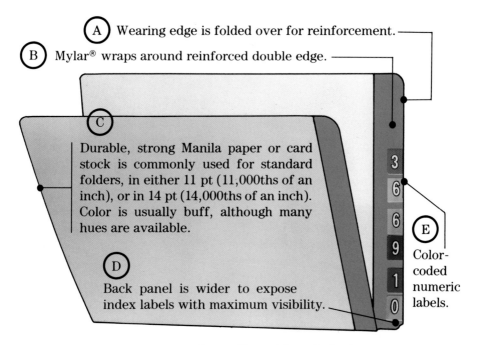

Ⓐ Wearing edge is folded over for reinforcement.

Ⓑ Mylar® wraps around reinforced double edge.

Ⓒ Durable, strong Manila paper or card stock is commonly used for standard folders, in either 11 pt (11,000ths of an inch), or in 14 pt (14,000ths of an inch). Color is usually buff, although many hues are available.

Ⓓ Back panel is wider to expose index labels with maximum visibility.

Ⓔ Color-coded numeric labels.

Typical good quality side tab folder.

Mylar is the registered trademark of Dupont de Nemours.

TOP TAB

The illustrations show various top-tab folders used with all types of drawer filing. They are classics and are popular because drawer filing is in general use. Sometimes drawer filing is called 'blind filing' — folders cannot be seen until the drawer is opened. Hence color coding for top-tab folders is less effective than with lateral filing.

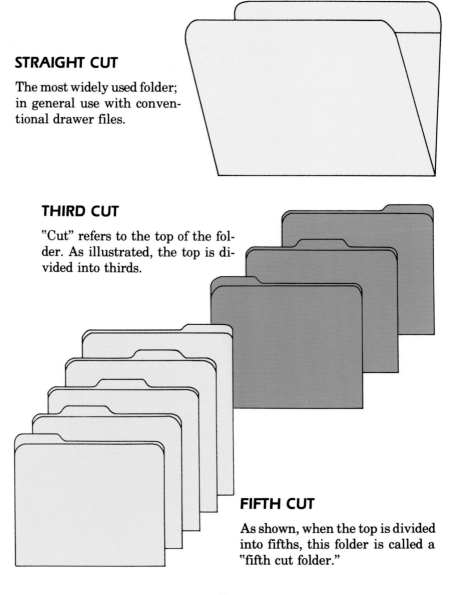

STRAIGHT CUT

The most widely used folder; in general use with conventional drawer files.

THIRD CUT

"Cut" refers to the top of the folder. As illustrated, the top is divided into thirds.

FIFTH CUT

As shown, when the top is divided into fifths, this folder is called a "fifth cut folder."

SIDE (or End) TAB FOLDERS

Side-tab folders are coming into ever wider use because of the trend to color-coded filing systems. It is easier and faster to file and to find them if color-coded. This saves labor — the costliest element of office costs. Illustrated are three popular types of side-tab folders.

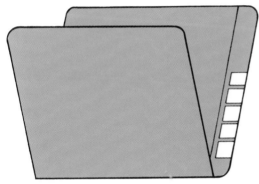

FULL END TAB

Illustrated is an end-tab folder that is reinforced with a double folder thickness. This is the most widely used folder for "shelf" filing.

NOTCHED END TAB

Here the bottom of the end tab is notched. It is mostly used with "roll-out" cabinets having a lip on the rollout shelf.

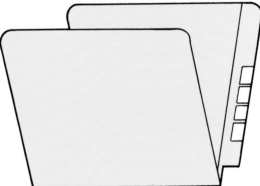

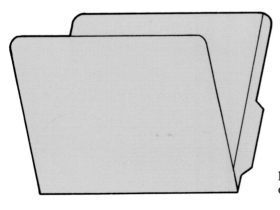

FOUR INCH BOTTOM TAB

A variation in common use is an end-tab folder with only the bottom four inches made into a tab. This leaves the upper part free for the full view of index guides.

CLASSIFICATION FOLDER

Here the folder is divided into subdivisions. This provides for the division of the contents of each folder into sub subjects. Front and back are pressboard, joined by a cloth or vinyl gusset.

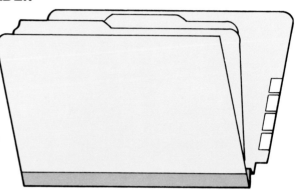

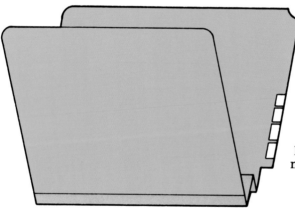

PRESSBOARD FOLDER

Sturdy pressboard is joined together with a cloth or vinyl gusset. This permits the filing of two or more inches of documents.

X-RAY JACKET

Color coding here is most effective in preventing loss, and in helping quick reference. The jacket is a sort of envelope open at the top. It is of a large size to accommodate x-rays.

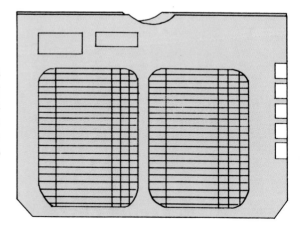

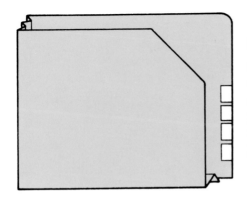

FILE POCKET

Open at one end, closed at the other. This enhances quick reference and easy filing. The file pocket is also made without the illustrated bottom and end expansion.

RED ROPE EXPANSION POCKET

Used when large groups of documents must be filed together. The expansion can be two, three, or four inches. The front and back are made of heavy "red rope" material instead of manila. The gusset is cloth or vinyl.

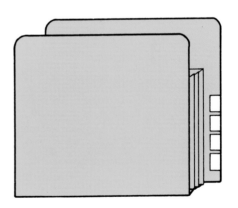

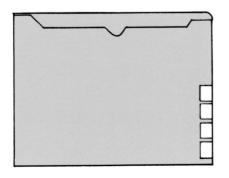

DENTAL POCKET

Widely used by dentists to file patient x-rays and histories. It is open at the top and is usually made with 11 pt manila.

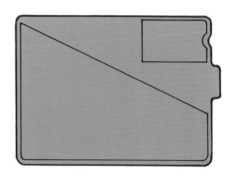

VINYL OUT-GUIDE

Made with heavy vinyl. The slash pockets are made with clear material to show any contents. The small top pocket is for an out card for the name of the person using the folder that is out-of-file.

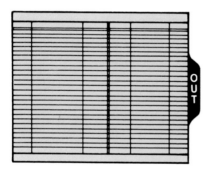

MANILA OUT-GUIDE

The manila guide is printed to show the name of the person "charged-out" with the file.

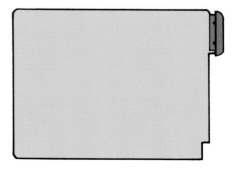

COLORVUE GUIDE

Used with open shelving to guide a person to a group of alphabetic or numeric files. The tab is made of plastic and is magnifying.

SUGGESTED READING

FILING SYSTEMS FOR INFORMATION MANAGEMENT
Marie E. Flatlie & Violet S. Thomas
John Wiley and Sons, New York, NY (1983)

RULES FOR ALPHABETIC FILING
Association of Records Managers and Administrators
4200 Somerset Drive, Suite 215
Prairie Village, KS 66208 (1985)

BUSINESS RECORDS CONTROL
Ernest D. Bassett, David G. Goodman, Joseph S. Fosegan
South-Western Publishing Company, Cincinnati, OH (1981)

FUNDAMENTAL FILING PRACTICE
Irene Place, Estelle L. Popham, Harry N. Fujita
Prentice-Hall, Englewood Cliffs, NJ (1973)

INFORMATION & RECORDS MANAGEMENT
Wilmer O. Maedke, Mary F. Robek, Gerald F. Brown
Glencoe Press, Encino, CA (1981)

INFORMATION RESOURCE MANAGEMENT
Betty R. Ricks & Kay E. Gow
South-Western Publishing Company, Cincinnati, OH (1984)

PROGRESSIVE FILING
Jeffrey Robert Stewart, Jr., Judith A. Scharle, Gilbert Kahn
McGraw-Hill Book Company, New York, NY (1980)

RECORDS MANAGEMENT: CONTROLLING BUSINESS INFORMATION
Irene Place & David J. Hyslop
Reston Publishing Company, Reston, VA (1982)

RECORDS MANAGEMENT
William Benedon
Prentice-Hall, Englewood Cliffs, NJ (1969)

RECORDS MANAGEMENT: SYSTEMS AND ADMINISTRATION
Violet S. Thomas, Dexter R. Schubert, and Jo Ann Lee
John Wiley and Sons, New York, NY (1983)

INDEX

*References to illustrations and photographs are printed in **boldface** type.*

ABOUT THE AUTHORS

Donald T. Barber, CA, CRM, CDP, is a well-known records management consultant. His career began in Canada as an internal auditor for a major tire and rubber company. His interest has always been in office systems. After service in the Canadian Navy he spent several years as consultant to a dozen major commercial businesses, replacing manual procedures with unit record systems.

He then became interested in records management with emphasis on developing and perfecting color-coded filing. Together with his long-time associate, Tom Scrymgeour, he invented the system known as Comp-u-color to produce color-coded labels for file folders. This became a stepping stone to a revolutionary microprocessor-controlled method of applying self-adhesive color-coded labels to file folders. This key unlocked a wealth of opportunity in modern filing systems.

Don Barber holds patents on a dozen related inventions, all designed to answer the need for filing system efficiency. He is truly a pioneer and an innovator in his field.

Dr. Mark Langemo, CRM, is a professor in the College of Business and Public Administration at the University of North Dakota where he received the "Teacher of the Year" award in 1984 for excellence in instruction. He is a recognized authority on records management, much sought after speaker, and dynamic seminar leader on management topics. He specializes in management and supervisory development and has published many thought-provoking articles on these subjects.

Dr. Langemo's work as a consultant has taken him to most of the states in the U.S.A., most of the provinces in Canada, and leading nations of Europe. His broad range of interests includes colleges and universities, government departments, corporations and health care organizations.

He has been honored by the Association of Records Managers and Administrators (ARMA) for distinguished contributions to records management. He is also a member of the Administrative Management Society, Office Systems Research Association, and other honorary and professional business organizations.

MARSDALE PUBLISHING CO.

A MEMO TO OUR READERS

As suggested by the title of this book, filing is a subject that is dynamic and ever changing. This book is a synthesis of the experiences of many filing practitioners, as noted in the acknowledgements.

We invite our readers to write to us with comments, suggestions, and experiences, so that future editions of *Filing Dynamics* will keep pace with the best and latest techniques and standards. It is with this kind of exchange of ideas that our profession will move ahead, and we wish to be a part of the progress.

Please write:

In USA — **MARSDALE PUBLISHING CO.**
3300 Powell St., Suite 5
Emeryville, California 94608

In Canada — 3080 Yonge Street, Suite 5035
Toronto, Ontario M4N 3N1